W0413480

# exercices

# L'ANGLAIS

## de A à Z

DESMOND O'SULLIVAN
M.A. Cantab

Avec la collaboration de :

MICHAEL SWAN
M.A. Oxon

FRANÇOISE HOUDART
Professeur agrégé d'anglais

HATIER

# AVANT-PROPOS

Ce livre d'exercices complète *L'anglais de A à Z*, mais il peut aussi s'utiliser indépendamment.
Il comprend :
- un test d'entrée *(Que savez-vous?)* et son corrigé,
- 190 exercices divisés en 31 unités grammaticales *(Pour progresser)*,
- le corrigé de tous les exercices.

***Le test***
Il porte essentiellement sur des points élémentaires. Son corrigé renvoie aux sections de *L'anglais de A à Z* pour les révisions et aux *Exercices A à Z* pour l'entraînement.

***Les exercices***
Ils abordent de nombreux points non inclus dans le test (élémentaires ou plus avancés). Ils illustrent, dans leur ensemble, l'essentiel de la grammaire anglaise, qu'ils font pratiquer d'une façon variée, vivante et créative.
Pour chaque exercice, sont précisés le point de grammaire sur lequel il porte et les sections de *L'anglais de A à Z* auxquelles il renvoie.
Dans certaines unités, des exercices de synthèse regroupent les points pratiqués séparément dans l'unité.

***Mode d'emploi suggéré***
• Faire d'abord le test et consulter le corrigé.
• Pour chaque réponse erronée, se reporter aux sections et exercices indiqués.
• Le lecteur pourra ensuite, selon ses préférences, faire systématiquement les autres exercices de chaque unité, ou bien sélectionner certains exercices pour résoudre des difficultés particulières.

---

© HATIER - Paris - 1994 - ISSN : 1140 0048 - ISBN : 2-218-**71802**-2

**S O M M A I R E** page

# Que savez-vous ?

***Entourez la bonne réponse.***

**1.** There's been ..... accident!
A a B an C the

**2.** My sister is ..... photographer.
A Ø B one C a

**3.** Are you interested in ..... nature?
A a B the C Ø

**4.** I take the bus .....
A every day B all days C every days

**5.** Don't forget to buy ..... milk.
A a B some C any

**6.** There's ..... butter on the table.
A any B no C not

**7.** You don't understand .....!!!
A nothing B something C anything

**8.** 'I've brought you ..... books.' 'Oh, thanks.'
A a few B few C a little

**9.** Do you have ..... time for me today?
A a little B a little of C a few

**10.** In general ..... people like children. I detest them!
A most of B most C most of the

**11.** We don't care if you go. We've got ..... friends!
**A** another **B** others **C** other

**12.** I don't know ..... men. Do you?
**A** this **B** that **C** those

**13.** 'Is this your car?' 'No, it's not .....'
**A** our **B** ours **C** to us

**14.** ..... coat is this?
**A** Who **B** Whom **C** Whose

**15.** ..... don't think this is correct.
**A** Me, I **B** For me, I **C** I

**16.** He's always looking at ..... in the mirror.
**A** himself **B** him **C** each other

**17.** The woman ..... phoned was American.
**A** who **B** whom **C** which

**18.** Do you have .....?
**A** colours differents **B** differents colours
**C** different colours

**19.** 'She's alone in the world now!' '.....!'
**A** The poor **B** Poor girl **C** Poor

**20.** She always gets ..... results than I do.
**A** best **B** good **C** better

**21.** That's ..... stupid question I've ever heard!
**A** the most **B** the more **C** most

**22.** He isn't ..... intelligent ..... you are.
**A** as … than **B** Ø … as **C** as … as

**23.** '..... you cold?' 'Yes, a little.'
**A** Have **B** Are **C** Do

**24.** Sorry. I can't ..... tomorrow.
**A** to come **B** come **C** coming

**25.** I hope that one day all nations ..... live in peace.
**A** could **B** will can **C** will be able to

**26.** He ..... come to the party. He's not sure.
A might B could C would

**27.** I ..... go to the dentist's last week.
A must B had to C will have to

**28.** You ..... smoke. It's bad for you.
A wouldn't B don't have to C shouldn't

**29.** We ..... now. It's getting late.
A had better go B would better go C had better to go

**30.** They ..... live in London. Now they live in Berlin.
A are used to B were used to C used to

**31.** I want ..... the manager.
A seeing B see C to see

**32.** She made me .....
A laugh B laughing C to laugh

**33.** We need money ..... on holiday.
A for go B for going C to go

**34.** I don't want ..... my mother.
A that he tells B him to tell C him tell

**35.** She's very ..... in astrology.
A interest B interesting C interested

**36.** They left without ..... goodbye.
A saying B to say C say

**37.** I would like ..... them.
A meet B to meet C meeting

**38.** Stop ..... so much noise.
A make B making C to make

**39.** She ..... us about once a month.
A visit B is visiting C visits

**40.** Don't talk to me. ..... to work!
A I try B I'm trying C I'll try

**41.** You didn't ..... your tea.
A drink B drunk C drank

**42.** We ..... to Rome last year. It was wonderful!
A are going B went C were going

**43.** He ..... the washing-up when she phoned.
A did B was doing C will do

**44.** Lucy ..... in the bath for two hours!
A reads B has read C has been reading

**45.** I ..... him since October.
A 've known B 've been knowing C know

**46.** Perhaps one day I ..... in another country.
A will live B would live C am living

**47.** We ..... her next Saturday at three o'clock.
A see B go to see C 're seeing

**48.** 'Bob – telephone!' 'I ..... !'
A go B 'll be going C 'll go

**49.** Our house ..... in 1920.
A built B was built C has built

**50.** ..... late yesterday?
A Did he arrive B Does he arrive C Did he arrived

**51.** What ..... after we left?
A did happen B happened C was happened

**52.** ..... lovely flowers!
A How B What C So

**53.** He's ..... good driver.
A a so B a such C such a

**54.** She likes it, .....?
A isn't it B isn't she C doesn't she

**55.** He ..... I was pretty.
A said me B told me C told to me

**56.** She said she ..... understand what I wanted.
**A** doesn't **B** didn't **C** hadn't

**57.** Can you tell me what time .....?
**A** the match starts **B** starts the match
**C** does the match start

**58.** If I had the time I ..... learn Chinese.
**A** will **B** shall **C** would

**59.** I'll write to her when I ..... her new address.
**A** will have **B** shall have **C** have

**60.** We ..... with them.
**A** often play tennis **B** play tennis often
**C** play often tennis

**61.** You speak .....
**A** well English **B** English well **C** English good

**62.** You never listen ..... me.
**A** at **B** Ø **C** to

**63.** 'When's your birthday?' 'It's ..... December.'
**A** on the tenth of **B** the ten **C** the ten of

**64.** Let's go ..... the cinema this evening!
**A** at **B** to **C** in

**65.** I haven't seen her .....
**A** for ten days **B** since ten days **C** ten days ago

**66.** She was ill ..... six weeks last year.
**A** during **B** for **C** while

**67.** He's only thirteen, but he talks ..... an adult.
**A** like **B** as **C** same as

**68.** I met her in the street .....
**A** there are two weeks **B** there are two weeks ago
**C** two weeks ago

**69.** I wish you ..... with me now!
**A** are **B** were **C** will be

**70.** She ..... with all my plans.
**A** is agree **B** agrees **C** is agreed

**71.** I asked ..... a policeman the way.
**A** Ø **B** at **C** to

**72.** Could you ..... how to get there?
**A** explain me **B** explain at me **C** explain to me

**73.** ..... your parents like?
**A** What **B** What are **C** How are

**74.** My grandmother ..... down the stairs last night.
**A** felt **B** fell **C** fallen

**75.** Where did you ..... it?
**A** live **B** left **C** leave

# Réponses

| Solution | Entraînement* | AZ** |
|---|---|---|
| **1.** B | **1.** 1 | 39, 41 |
| **2.** C | **1.** 2 | 40.1, 270.1 |
| **3.** C | **1.** 3 | 42 |
| **4.** A | **2.** 1 | 20 |
| **5.** B | **2.** 5 | 365, 256 |
| **6.** B | **2.** 7 | 260 |
| **7.** C | **2.** 9 | 366, 261 |
| **8.** A | **3.** 1 | 222 |
| **9.** A | **3.** 1 | 222 |
| **10.** B | **3.** 6 | 239 |
| **11.** C | **3.** 5 | 33, 277 |
| **12.** C | **4.** 1 | 385 |
| **13.** B | **4.** 2 | 297, 298 |
| **14.** C | **5.** 2 | 299, 408 |
| **15.** C | **7.** 2 | 320.2 |
| **16.** A | **7.** 3 | 325, 114 |
| **17.** A | **7.** 8 | 326 |
| **18.** C | **8.** 1 | 7 |
| **19.** B | **8.** 3 | 12 |
| **20.** C | **9.** 1 | 80, 82 |
| **21.** A | **9.** 4 | 80, 88, 90 |
| **22.** C | **9.** 5 | 44, 381 |
| **23.** B | **10.** 2 | 61 |
| **24.** B | **11.** 3 | 72, 73 |
| **25.** C | **11.** 3 | 72, 62 |
| **26.** A | **11.** 5 | 232, 73, 92 |
| **27.** B | **12.** 1 | 244 |
| **28.** C | **12.** 4 | 353, 357, 102 |
| **29.** A | **13.** 1 | 164 |
| **30.** C | **13.** 3 | 393, 395 |
| **31.** C | **14.** 1 | 193 |
| **32.** A | **14.** 1 | 194 |
| **33.** C | **14.** 3 | 196 |
| **34.** B | **14.** 4 | 197 |
| **35.** C | **15.** 1 | 115 |
| **36.** A | **15.** 5 | 202 |

*Ces numéros renvoient aux unités et aux exercices de ce livre.
**Ces numéros renvoient aux sections de *Pratique de l'anglais de A à Z*.

| | | |
|---|---|---|
| **37.** B | **16.** 1 | 220, 201 |
| **38.** B | **16.** 3, 4 | 370 |
| **39.** C | **17.** 1 | 307, 308 |
| **40.** B | **17.** 2 | 309, 310 |
| **41.** A | **18.** 1, 3 | 316 |
| **42.** B | **18.** 1, 3 | 316, 317 |
| **43.** B | **18.** 2 | 318 |
| **44.** C | **18.** 5 | 314, 100 |
| **45.** A | **18.** 6 | 314 |
| **46.** A | **19.** 1 | 149, 91 |
| **47.** C | **19.** 3 | 151 |
| **48.** C | **19.** 4 | 152 |
| **49.** B | **20.** 2 | 281, 282 |
| **50.** A | **21.** 1 | 339 |
| **51.** B | **21.** 1 | 339, 166 |
| **52.** B | **21.** 7 | 132, 362 |
| **53.** C | **26.** 4 | 362 |
| **54.** C | **22.** 1, 2 | 375 |
| **55.** B | **23.** 5 | 349 |
| **56.** B | **23.** 1 | 103 |
| **57.** A | **23.** 3 | 104 |
| **58.** C | **24.** 1 | 186 |
| **59.** C | **25.** 1 | 405 |
| **60.** A | **26.** 1 | 290 |
| **61.** B | **26.** 3 | 292 |
| **62.** C | **27.** 1 | 304.2 |
| **63.** A | **27.** 3 | 53, 97 |
| **64.** B | **27.** 3 | 54 |
| **65.** A | **18.** 2 | 100, 18 |
| **66.** B | **27.** 6 | 111, 112 |
| **67.** A | **28.** 2 | 45, 348 |
| **68.** C | **29.** 2 | 18, 189 |
| **69.** B | **30.** 1 | 411.1 |
| **70.** B | **30.** 3 | 19 |
| **71.** A | **30.** 3 | 50 |
| **72.** C | **30.** 3 | 134 |
| **73.** B | **31** | 180 |
| **74.** B | **31** | 241 |
| **75.** C | **31** | 241 |

# À Z Pour progresser

## 1 Déterminants : articles

**A / AN** ; NOMS INDÉNOMBRABLES *(AZ 39, 256)*

***1. Répartissez les mots ci-dessous entre* a, an *et* Ø.**

| | | | | |
|---|---|---|---|---|
| beautiful overcoat | easy question | excellent Chinese | | |
| great honour | headache | heavy rain | honest man | |
| hospital | hour | icy water | information | invitation |
| machines | new furniture | opinion | student | stupidity |
| uniform | unusual name | | | |

*a*: *beautiful overcoat, ...*

*an*: .............

Ø: .............

**A / AN** (CAS PARTICULIERS) *(AZ 40)*

***2. Récrivez les phrases erronées.***

1. My sister's architect.
2. Unfortunately she was without job for six months.
3. She got £40 a week from the government.
4. She lives in an expensive house in Oxford.
5. Now she works as teacher in London.
6. It's quite interesting job.
7. But it's such long journey from Oxford.
8. What pity!
9. She was a good architect.
10. It's lucky she's still got sense of humour.

THE (LES GÉNÉRALISATIONS) *(AZ 42)*

***3. Barrez** the **là où il ne convient pas.***

1. All you need is the love.
2. The service in this restaurant is terrible.
3. The violence is a big problem in the modern society.
4. I've heard her on the radio but I've never seen her on the TV.
5. I find the country rather boring.
6. The inflation has increased by two per cent this year.
7. The cinema in this country is getting better.
8. The Irish coffee is always made with the Irish whiskey.
9. The CD was invented in Japan and Holland.

**THE ; LAST ... ; NEXT ...** *(AZ 43, 217, 250)*

***4. Mettez** the **ou Ø, selon le cas.***

1. They're meeting ..... Paul's sister ..... next Tuesday at ..... Waterloo station.
2. Did you know that ..... President Clinton studied at ..... Oxford University for a year?
3. According to ..... latest forecast *(= la météo)* the weather is going to be good for ..... next five days.
4. I usually have a sandwich for ..... lunch. Then I have a proper meal at ..... dinner.
5. Ann and I played ..... golf ..... last weekend.
6. Why are you learning ..... Dutch? Everyone speaks ..... English in ..... Netherlands.
7. ..... next year we're going to climb ..... Mont Blanc.
8. The man had ..... brown eyes and ..... dark hair.
9. 'Have you read ..... latest Roddy Doyle novel?' 'No. I didn't enjoy ..... last one I read.'
10. She goes to ..... school on ..... Mondays by ..... car, but every other day she goes by ..... train.
11. I haven't slept very well ..... last two nights.
12. Tom is in ..... hospital. Mary is at ..... university. Bob is at ..... home. I'm the only one at ..... work!

EXERCICE DE SYNTHÈSE *(AZ 39-43, 217, 250, 256)*

***5. Reconstituez ce fait divers en ajoutant** a/ an, the **ou Ø.***

**'Goodbye Mum!'**

..(1).. last month Ann and Tony were enjoying ..(2).. dinner at ..(3).. expensive restaurant, with ..(4).. romantic music and ..(5).. wonderful food. They were on holiday, and ..(6).. love was in the air. Ann and Tom were having their dessert when they noticed ..(7).. old lady sitting by herself at another table. ..(8).. lady smiled at them, and they smiled politely back. ..(9).. next moment the old lady stood up and came across to their table.

'What ..(10).. lovely dress!' she remarked to Ann. 'It's ..(11).. pity it brings me ..(12).. unhappy memories. My daughter used to wear something like that, but she was killed ..(13).. last year in ..(14).. Italy. ..(15).. last few months have been very hard for me. ..(16).. life can be very cruel.' She had ..(17).. blue eyes, and at this moment they filled with ..(18).. tears *(= larmes)*. 'Would you do something for me, please?' she said quietly. 'It would make me very happy if you would say "Goodbye, Mum" when I am leaving ..(19).. restaurant.'

Of course Ann and Tom immediately agreed, and when in ..(20).. next few minutes she stood up from her table to go, they both said goodbye to 'Mum'.

Soon afterwards Tom asked to pay. 'There must be ..(21).. mistake,' he said when he saw ..(22).. total.

'No,' said ..(23).. waiter. 'It includes ..(24).. cost of ..(25).. old lady's dinner. She said that her daughter would pay.'

(*The Guardian* – adapté)

## 2 Déterminants : *all, both, some, ...*

**ALL** ET **EVERY** ; **EACH** ET **EVERY** ; TOUT *(AZ 20, 113, 388)*

***1. Mettez*** all, each ***ou*** every. ***Dans certains cas, il y a deux possibilités.***

1. ..... day is the same in this job.
2. Are you going to stay in the bath ..... day?!!
3. We walk to school together ..... morning.
4. I get worried ..... time I think about her.
5. Detective Timms wants to talk to ..... person individually.
6. I haven't had any sleep at all. The baby hasn't stopped crying ..... night!
7. ..... employee has his or her own identity card.
8. My brother and my sister have ..... got two children.
9. ..... parent wants the best for his or her children.
10. They both work for the same bank, but ..... of them is in a different branch.
11. ..... hotel in the town was full.
12. Close your eyes. Now open ..... one slowly: first the left, then the right.

**ALL** ET **EVERYTHING** ; **ALL** ET **WHOLE** *(AZ 21, 22)*

***2. Complétez par*** all, everything ***ou*** (the) whole***.***

1. 'They've spent ..... their money.' 'They can't have spent .....!' 'Yes, they have. They spent the ..... lot on computer games and videos.' 'A ..... month's pocket money?' 'Yes, .....!'
2. 'How do you feel?' 'My ..... body hurts. ..... the muscles in my legs are in torture. The ..... team *(= équipe)* feels the same.' 'I'm not surprised. You didn't stop running for the ..... of the match.'
3. 'Is the presentation ready?' 'Yes and no. I spent ..... of Monday collecting the information, then a ..... day on Tuesday preparing the documentation. I had almost finished the ..... thing when something happened to the computer. ..... the information was destroyed. I lost .....!!!'

**BOTH** *(AZ 67)*

***3. Remettez les éléments des phrases suivantes dans un ordre correct.***

1. were / the / locked / Both / doors .
2. men / love / She / in / both / was / with .
3. Irish / and / Niamh / are / Donal / names / both .
4. from / grandfather / my / my / Both / grandmother / and / Russia / came .
5. both / He / piano / and / plays / the / sings .
6. inexpensive / flat / both / and / is / This / spacious .
7. in / them / Both / live / Canada / of .
8. music / enjoy / I / modern / both / and / music / classical .

**EITHER** ET **NEITHER** + NOM *(AZ 116)*

***4. Reliez les phrases à l'aide de*** either ***ou*** neither***.***

**Ex. :** You can use my car. You can use her car.
*You can use either car.*
**Ex. :** This pen doesn't work. That pen doesn't work.
*Neither pen works.*

1. She doesn't want this one. She doesn't want that one.
2. I can't speak Spanish. He can't speak Spanish.
3. We can't come this weekend. We can't come next weekend.
4. My younger sister doesn't like jazz. My older sister doesn't like jazz.
5. My father doesn't eat meat. My mother doesn't eat meat. (Utilisez *parents.*)
6. We could go to Greece. We could go to Italy. (Utilisez *country.*)

**SOME** ET **ANY** *(AZ 365)*

***5. Complétez par*** some***,*** any ***ou*** Ø***.***

1. 'Have you got ..... apples?' 'Sorry, we haven't got ..... apples, but we do have ..... very nice bananas. Or would you like ..... oranges?' 'Could I have ..... bananas, please? Two kilos.'
2. 'I've hardly ..... money left. Have you got .....?' 'You never have ..... money! Well, I haven't got ..... either! And even if I did have ...., I wouldn't give you ..... of it!'

→

3. I found the house without ..... difficulty.
4. If I had ..... time, I'd redecorate *(= repeindre)* the whole house myself.
5. 'You've got ..... wonderful teeth *(= dents).*' 'And you've got ..... very bad eyes! Look – they're false!!'

**OF** APRÈS **SOME, ...**; **BOTH**; **EITHER** *(AZ 265, 67, 116)*

***6. Barrez*** of ***là où il ne convient pas.***

1. Some of you know me already.
2. Both of men had red hair.
3. Neither of these pens are mine.
4. All of this will be yours one day.
5. Unfortunately, both of us forgot.
6. Some of modern art is hard to understand.
7. She doesn't want either of them.

**NOT ... ANY, NOT ... A, NO, NONE** *(AZ 260)*

***7. Rendez les phrases suivantes négatives en utilisant*** not ... any, not ... a, no ***et*** none. ***Lorsqu'il y a deux possibilités, mettez-les toutes les deux.***

1. There are some new students.
2. She wants some more soup.
3. He's got a car.
4. All of us know how to ski.
5. They've got some children.
6. All of these people can speak Arabic.
7. There's some cheese in the fridge.
8. I had a headache.
9. We've got some time left.

**ANY** (= N'IMPORTE QUEL) *(AZ 34)*

***8. Complétez par*** any, anybody, anything ***ou*** anywhere.

1. ..... could see that he was lying.
2. 'What shall I tell her?' 'Just say .....'
3. ..... time after 7 pm is usually OK for me.
4. ..... is warmer than here.
5. In this situation ..... could happen!
6. She can play ..... instrument.

7. He's very friendly: he'll talk to .....
8. Don't worry about me. I can sleep .....

**SOME, ...** : COMPOSÉS ; **NOT ... ANYTHING, ...** *(AZ 366, 261)*

***9. Complétez les phrases par les composés de*** some***,*** any***,*** every ***et*** no***.***

1. 'I think there's ..... at the door.' 'Oh, it's probably Ann.'
2. 'Is ..... here yet?' 'No, we're still waiting for Tom.'
3. I can't find my keys ..... Has ..... seen them?
4. 'Where are you going on holiday?' '..... We're staying here.'
5. We didn't know. ..... told us .....
6. 'Did you hear .....?' 'No, .....' 'I think there's ..... out there.' 'What?' 'I don't know, but it's ..... behind those trees.'
7. 'Did ..... telephone?' 'No, .....' 'There's ..... wrong, isn't there?' 'No, ..... is fine. There's ..... to worry about.' 'I don't believe you. ..... is wrong!'

EXERCICE DE SYNTHÈSE

***10. Corrigez les phrases suivantes.***

1. I stayed with her all the day. *(AZ 20)*
2. At every time she visited us she brought us presents. *(AZ 20)*
3. Not everybody isn't as generous as her. *(AZ 20)*
4. We come here every days. *(AZ 20)*
5. She wore different coloured socks on every foot. *(AZ 113)*
6. Toys, money, a good education – we gave our children all! *(AZ 21)*
7. He stayed all a month. *(AZ 22)*
8. David and John play both football. *(AZ 67)*
9. His parents speak and Spanish and French. *(AZ 67)*
10. 'Tea or coffee?' 'Either, thanks. I'm not thirsty.' *(AZ 116)*
11. Our teacher didn't accept neither of our excuses. *(AZ 116)*
12. Sorry, we haven't got some time. *(AZ 365)*
13. Would you put any milk in my tea, please? *(AZ 365)*
14. He's got some very long fingers. *(AZ 365)*
15. She hasn't got any cat. *(AZ 365)*
16. You can visit us all day that you are free. *(AZ 34)*
17. A disaster could happen at all moment. *(AZ 34)*
18. Everybody are waiting. *(AZ 366)*
19. We've never travelled nowhere in our lives. *(AZ 366)*

# 3 Déterminants : *little, few, much, …*

A LITTLE, A FEW, LITTLE, FEW, A BIT *(AZ 222)*

***1. Traduisez en anglais.***

1. Un peu de vin, madame?
2. Elle a eu quelques problèmes avec son mari. (present perfect)
3. Je l'ai vue quelques fois. Nous avons passé quelque temps ensemble. (present perfect)
4. Ils ont été un peu stupides. (present perfect)
5. Nous aurons besoin de pas mal d'argent.
6. "Est-ce que vous avez beaucoup d'étudiants?" "Oui, pas mal."
7. Peu de parents comprennent leurs enfants.
8. Il nous reste très peu de temps. *(We have … left.)*

MUCH, … ; A LOT (OF), … *(AZ 243, 227)*

***2. Mettez*** much ***ou*** many ***lorsque c'est possible,*** a lot (of) ***ou*** lots (of) ***dans les autres cas.***

1. He hasn't got ..... friends.
2. We haven't received ..... news from them.
3. 'Is there any pollution?' 'Not .....'
4. 'Did you see any tigers?' 'Not .....'
5. We don't go out ..... these days.
6. He's had ..... girlfriends but he's never been married.
7. There's too ..... noise in there.
8. We've had so ..... problems this year.
9. She drinks .....
10. ..... time has been wasted on this.
11. ..... people are coming to my party.
12. 'Has she had any experience?' 'Yes, quite .....'

HOW MUCH …?; SO MUCH; TOO MUCH *(AZ 183, 363, 390)*

***3. Complétez les phrases par*** how much/ many, so much/ many ***ou*** too much/ many***.***

1. ..... time have they got?
2. There are ..... countries that I want to visit.
3. Sorry, I can't come. I've got ..... work to do.

4. It's wonderful: they love each other .....!
5. ..... rooms are there in the house?
6. 'He doesn't look very well.' 'I think he's had ..... to drink.'
7. 'And we need some sugar.' '.....?' 'Two kilos.'
8. ..... needs repairing in the house – it's going to be a big job!
9. 'Mum, how many stars are there?' 'I don't know. ..... to count!'
10. 'Apparently a lot of people were killed.' 'Really? .....?'

TROP ; **ENOUGH** *(AZ 390, 126)*

***4. Complétez par*** too***,*** too much/ many (of) ***ou*** enough (of)***.***

1. She works ..... hard. She never takes a holiday.
2. 'Why didn't you buy that blue dress?' 'It wasn't big .....'
3. There are ..... cars on the roads these days. It's terrible.
4. They didn't study hard ..... to pass their exams.
5. I don't think we've got ..... those special instruments.
6. Are there going to be ..... people to carry everything?
7. She didn't finish all her homework – there was ..... it.
8. You watch ..... TV. That's why you get headaches.
9. Will you be well ..... to play on Saturday?
10. It's ..... wet to go for a walk. Let's stay inside.
11. I feel sick. I think I ate ..... Sarah's cream cakes!

**ANOTHER ; OTHER(S)** *(AZ 33, 277)*

***5. Complétez par*** another***,*** other ***ou*** others***.***

1. Yes, I know Brigit, but who is the ..... woman next to her?
2. 'She's seeing ..... man.' 'Does her boyfriend know?'
3. Tim and Mary put the children to bed while the ..... did the cooking.
4. Sue and Meg are watching TV. The ..... girls are out.
5. 'You've already had six whiskies.' 'Only six? Give me .....!'
6. We still need ..... two players.
7. We don't like these curtains. Could you show us some .....?
8. I've found one of my black shoes, but I can't find the .....

**OF** APRÈS **MOST ; ENOUGH ;** TROP *(AZ 239, 126, 390)*

***6. Barrez*** of ***là où il ne convient pas.***

1. I do like opera. It's just that I haven't heard enough of it.
2. We haven't got much of petrol left.
3. Perhaps we've got too many of those red decorations.
4. Many of people in this city are out of work.
5. Have you had enough of meat?
6. Most of this book is very interesting.
7. He didn't have too much of difficulty finding us.
8. Much of Manchester is quite modern.
9. Most of homes in Britain have a television.
10. Most of people want a quiet life.

# 4 Démonstratifs et possessifs

DÉMONSTRATIFS *(AZ 385)*

***1. Mettez*** this**,** that**,** these ***ou*** those**.**

1. Just look at ..... car over there!
2. I'm so happy! I'll remember ..... day for the rest of my life.
3. 'Who are ..... men at the bus stop?' 'Sorry, where?'
4. ..... stamps here come from Ecuador.
5. 'He sent me some flowers.' '..... was nice of him.'
6. 'I think ..... books will interest you.' 'Oh, thanks.'
7. Come here. I want you to look at ..... It's really incredible!
8. In ..... days not many people had cars, so they had to walk.
9. I'll never forget ..... moment when I broke my leg.
10. And where are you living ..... days?

POSSESSIFS : ADJECTIFS, PRONOMS *(AZ 297, 298, 300)*

***2. Choisissez la réponse qui convient.***

1. That's Mary. *Her/ His* brother is in my class.
2. We're going to sell *our/ ours* house.
3. 'Is that *your/ yours* pen?' 'No, it's *her/ hers*.'
4. My/Mine is red. *Their/ Theirs* is white.
5. One should trust *one/ one's* heart.
6. I broke *my/ the* arm in the accident.
7. He put *his/ the* hand up because he knew the answer.
8. Now children, please open *your book/ your books* at page 1.
9. Mrs Jones is a colleague of *him/ his*.
10. I'm a friend of *your mother/ your mother's*.

CAS POSSESSIF : FORMATION ET EMPLOI *(AZ 301, 302)*

***3. Pour compléter les phrases suivantes, utilisez les mots et expressions ci-dessous au cas possessif. Il y a parfois plusieurs possibilités.***

| | | | | | |
|---|---|---|---|---|---|
| Ann | dentist | dog | Joe and Sue | Jones | men |
| old woman | President of Ireland | Saturday | students | | |
| young children | | | | | |

1. 'The ..... dinner looks disgusting.' 'Maybe, but Snoopy likes it.'
2. ..... coats are upstairs in the bedroom, with their hats.
3. We're going to buy the ..... car. They want to buy a new one.
4. Are you ..... husband?
5. ..... opinions about the world are often more interesting than their parents'.
6. The ..... visit to the United Nations will take place in May.
7. Tom and Bob are having a shower *(= douche)* in the ..... changing room.
8. My tooth hurts. I'm going to the ..... this afternoon.
9. Are you playing in ..... match?
10. I still haven't corrected the ..... homework.
11. The ..... face seemed familiar.

CAS POSSESSIF : FORMATION ET EMPLOI *(AZ 301, 302)*

***4. Corrigez les phrases suivantes.***

1. Those are the Veronica's CDs.
2. Are you the womens' representative?
3. I'm the Head's of Department secretary.
4. These are Paul's and Sarah toothbrushes.
5. 'Whose office is this?' 'Alans.'
6. She's at the doctor at the moment.
7. Are you going to Mike and Linda tonight?
8. He broke the chair's back.
9. It was a Shakespeare's play.
10. That's the baby's mother that was kidnapped.
11. Have you been to the Matisse's exhibition?

# 5 Mots interrogatifs

**WHAT…?** ET **WHICH …?** *(AZ 404)*

***1. Mettez*** what ***ou*** which.

1. ..... is the capital of Peru?
2. Quito, Bogota, or Lima – ..... is it?
3. '..... are your bags?' 'The brown ones.'
4. ..... size shoes *(= pointure de chaussures)* do you take?
5. ..... sorts of CDs have they got?
6. ..... car is yours – this one or the other one?

**WHOSE?** *(AZ 299)*

***2. Utilisez*** Whose…? ***pour poser les questions correspondant aux réponses suivantes. (Sous deux formes lorsque c'est possible.)***

1. That's Tom's bicycle.
2. Those are our books.
3. This is my uncle's house.
4. These are Ann's children.
5. It's their dog.
6. I'm going to my brother's wedding.

**WHO?** ET **WHOM?** *(AZ 408)*

***3. Posez des questions portant sur les mots en italique.***

1. *Tom* lives in that house.
2. I spoke to *her husband.*
3. They were with *their parents.*
4. We saw *Sue and Sally.*
5. *John* has just got married.
6. I don't like *Peter.*
7. They gave the money to *Ann.*
8. She's standing in front of *Bob.*

NOMS : PLURIEL ; **PERSON** ET **PEOPLE** *(AZ 254, 288)*

***1. Classez les noms ci-dessous selon leur forme au pluriel.***

| |
|---|
| bath bird box brush chair chief child country crisis data factory fish flat foot glass grown-up house key knife passer-by penny person phenomenon potato roof sheep sock tooth toy watch wife woman judge |

car**s** : *baths*, …
bus**es** : *boxes*, …
bab**ies** : *countries*, …
hal**ves** : *knives*, …
Autre forme : *children*, …

NOMS : EMPLOI *(AZ 255, 256)*

***2. Choisissez la forme qui convient.***

1. The team have won all *its/ their* matches.
2. *A/ Ø* loud music was coming from the flat above.
3. Ten kilometres *is/ are* not very far.
4. They had *a/ Ø* very wet weather.
5. Sorry, I can't stop. I'm in *a/ Ø* hurry.
6. Let me give you *an advice/ a piece of* advice.
7. The police *is / are* looking for a tall man with fair hair.
8. This book is written in *a/ Ø* very simple English.
9. I'm afraid the news *is/ are* not very good.
10. Politics *has/ have* always been a very dirty business.
11. Spaghetti *is/ are* difficult to eat.
12. *This/ These* series of books *is/ are* very useful.
13. His jeans *was/ were* very old.
14. The luggage *hasn't/ haven't* arrived yet.

NOMS COMPOSÉS *(AZ 258)*

***3. Construisez dix noms composés en combinant les éléments des deux listes (il y a parfois plusieurs possibilités). Puis, mettez-les au pluriel.***

**Ex.** : *art gallery (art galleries)*

| |
|---|
| art business fish jeans living news police sports tennis three-day ticket time toilet traffic woman |

| |
|---|
| astronaut bag gallery journey light man market match office paper programme room shop station table |

## 7 Les pronoms

ONE(S) *(AZ 269)*

***1. Complétez par*** one, ones ***ou Ø.***

1. Can I try the red dress on? I don't like the blue .....
2. I've got some black shoes, but I haven't got any brown .....
3. 'Do you want white sugar or brown sugar?' 'Brown ....., please.'
4. 'Which are your bags?' 'The ..... over there.'
5. I don't like milk chocolate but I love dark .....
6. That's my house – the ..... on the left.
7. You've got a much bigger ..... than I have!

PRONOMS PERSONNELS SUJETS ET COMPLÉMENTS *(AZ 320, 321)*

***2. Corrigez les phrases suivantes.***

1. My friend, she works in a factory.
2. Joe and Tom, they are brothers.
3. The subject that he enjoys least, it is mathematics.
4. Don't worry – it's us who'll do it!
5. With my boyfriend, we are getting married.
6. They live in a house. Me, I live in a flat.
7. Shall I turn off it?
8. Can you describe me the man?
9. Tell to Brigit that lunch is ready.
10. Jack is still too young to dress him. *(him = Jack)*

PRONOMS RÉFLÉCHIS ; **EACH OTHER ...** *(AZ 325, 114)*

***3. Complétez par des pronoms réfléchis ou*** each other / one another.

1. 'What are we doing here?' 'I've been asking ..... the same question!'
2. My grandmother can't look after ..... any more.
3. Our parents don't talk to ..... these days.
4. One has to defend .....
5. My brother and I always help ..... if we are in difficulty.
6. 'Our television is broken.' 'Oh, we had the same problem ..... last week.'
7. They managed to do it by .....
8. My sister and I often wear ..... clothes.
9. She told him to make ..... at home.
10. They looked at ..... without saying a word.

C'EST *(AZ 323)*

***4. Complétez par*** it, that / this, he ***ou*** she. ***Il y a parfois plusieurs réponses possibles.***

1. The phone rang. ..... was my mother.
2. 'Who's Margaret?' '.....'s my sister.'
3. .....'s a very friendly little boy.
4. 'What's this?' '.....'s my fax machine.'
5. It's Sunday – .....'s why I'm not at work!
6. 'Who was at the door?' '..... was only the postman.'
7. Gloria walked towards me. ..... was a tall woman with dark eyes.
8. Someone called my name. ..... was Andy.

**THEY = HE OR SHE** *(AZ 324)*

***5. Complétez par*** they, them, themselves ***ou*** their.

1. No one should take ..... too seriously.
2. Everyone did ..... best.
3. Somebody's been smoking in here, haven't .....?
4. You want a young person so you can pay ..... less!
5. Everybody can do what ..... want to.
6. I hope nobody has hurt .....
7. If anybody says anything to you, just tell ..... to go away.
8. Someone hasn't finished ..... dinner!

ON *(AZ 268.1, 2, 3)*

***6. Traduisez en anglais.***

1. On ne peut pas toujours avoir raison *(= be right)*.
2. En Autriche *(= Austria)* on parle l'allemand.
3. On l'exprime autrement *(= in a different way)* en français.
4. Où est-ce qu'on va ce soir?
5. On n'a jamais assez de temps dans la vie pour tout faire!
6. On est arrivé très tard. (prétérit)
7. À Paris on est toujours pressé *(= in a hurry)*!
8. On ne joue pas beaucoup au football aux États-Unis.

ON *(AZ 268.4, 5 ; 282)*

***7. Traduisez en anglais.***

1. On a changé mon numéro de téléphone.
2. On t'attend en bas *(= downstairs)*. Un monsieur ...
3. On a construit *(= build)* la maison il y a trente ans.
4. Paul! On t'appelle!
5. On vous enverra l'argent.
6. On a volé mon sac!
7. On m'a envoyé des fleurs!

**WHO(M)** ET **WHICH ; THAT** *(AZ 326, 327)*

***8. Complétez par*** who, which, that ***ou Ø.***

1. He's the man ..... stole my bicycle!
2. That's the chair ..... is broken.
3. Is there anything ..... they want from the shops?
4. Golf? There's nothing ..... bores me more!
5. Is she the girl ..... he likes so much?
6. Here's something ..... will make you laugh!
7. There are the keys ..... you were looking for.
8. Try to remember everything ..... he told you.
9. What's the biggest animal ..... has ever lived?

CE QUI, CE QUE *(AZ 328)*

***9. Choisissez la forme qui convient (***what, which ***ou*** that***).***

1. *What/ Which* I like about her is her sense of humour.
2. In his job he travels a lot, *what/ which* he really enjoys.
3. We've done all *that/ what* you asked us to do.

→

4. She isn't married, *what/ which* surprised me.
5. You'd better give him *what/ which* he wants!
6. All *that/ what* matters is that you love her.
7. I passed all my exams, *what/ which* pleased my parents.
8. *What/ Which* I detest is wasting time.
9. Everything *that/ what* goes wrong is always my fault!

WHOSE ET **OF WHICH** ; DONT *(AZ 329, 109)*

***10. Corrigez ou améliorez les phrases suivantes.***

1. He's someone whose I can never remember the name.
2. Isn't she the woman whose the husband left her?
3. It's a job of which the value is often underestimated.
4. She was a person whose everyone was jealous of.
5. It's dogs of which he's afraid.
6. He's a man of whom you need to be careful.
7. We've got three children, of whom two are still at school.
8. He wrote a lot of novels, of which the most famous are perhaps *Nana* and *Germinal*.

PRÉPOSITION + QUI / LEQUEL *(AZ 330)*

***11. Transformez les phrases pour les rendre moins formelles.***

**Ex. :** Is this the picture at which you were looking?
*Is this the picture you were looking at?*

1. She's the woman for whom we work.
2. Are these the books in which he is interested?
3. This is the family with whom I stayed.
4. Here's the hole *(= trou)* out of which the rat came.
5. He's the man to whom she's getting married.
6. This is the problem about which they are worried.
7. They are the people against whom we are playing.

NON EMPLOI DE **THAT** *(AZ 331)*

***12. Ajoutez un pronom relatif là où c'est nécessaire. Mettez des virgules lorsqu'il en faut.***

1. The man I spoke to was called Smith.
2. The journey was very uncomfortable lasted ten hours.
3. The people live downstairs are French.

4. My brother has a house in Cambridge works in London.
5. The house we bought cost a lot of money.
6. The car is outside belongs to my neighbour.
7. Tom you met last night is moving to the USA next month.

## 8 Les adjectifs

ADJECTIFS : PLACE ET ACCORD ; ORDRE ; **AND** *(AZ 7-9)*

***1. Corrigez les phrases suivantes.***

1. This is a story very exciting.
2. These questions are very difficults.
3. Are you going to the vegetables market?
4. Worried, I asked her where she had been.
5. Why don't you wear your cotton white dress?
6. I've just bought a leather expensive jacket.
7. Isn't he an American famous film star?
8. She's got black beautiful hair.
9. The two last days have been very tiring.
10. He was wearing a long and heavy coat.
11. What do you think of that aluminium, glass table?
12. He was young, rich, good-looking.

ADJECTIFS COMPOSÉS *(AZ 11)*

***2. Transformez les phrases suivantes en construisant des adjectifs composés.***

**Ex. :** He always dressed very well.
*He was always very well-dressed.*

1. He likes people whose minds are open.
2. I asked a policeman who looked friendly.
3. She's got a very good nature. *(She is ...)*
4. The soldiers moved towards the crowd which was throwing stones.
5. 'What colour was it?' 'Between blue and green.'
6. I generally use my right hand.
7. A herbivore is an animal that eats plants.

**3. *Traduisez en anglais.***

1. "Il a perdu sa femme." "Le pauvre!"
2. Nous travaillons beaucoup avec les handicappés.
3. L'important, c'est de s'amuser *(= have a good time)* !
4. Les riches doivent payer plus d'impôts *(= taxes)* que les pauvres.
5. Un aveugle a été attaqué hier par deux jeunes.
6. On dit que *(= It is said that)* les Irlandais sont très musiciens *(= musical)*.
7. Elle a une Japonaise et six Français dans sa classe d'anglais.
8. Le gouvernement ne s'intéresse pas beaucoup *(= is not very interested in)* aux chômeurs.
9. Quels sont les principaux besoins *(= the main needs)* des malades mentaux?
10. Je n'aime pas les égoïstes.

# 9 La comparaison

PLUS … QUE, LE PLUS … *(AZ 80-82)*

***1. Mettez les mots entre parenthèses au comparatif ou au superlatif, selon le sens.***

1. Cairo is *(old)* than New York – and it's *(noisy)*!
2. English is *(easy)* to learn than French, but Esperanto is the *(easy)* language of all!
3. This shop has all the *(late)* CDs. *(AZ 217)*
4. That's the *(big)* sandwich I've ever seen!
5. This is the *(happy)* day of my life!
6. Men think they are *(intelligent)* than women – which proves that they aren't!
7. This is the *(expensive)* restaurant in town.
8. If you're going to succeed, you're going to have to work a lot *(hard)* this year!
9. This has been the *(bad)* winter for fifty years.
10. There are *(many)* sheep in New Zealand than people.
11. My *(old)* brother is two years *(old)* than me. He's a year *(young)* than my sister. She's the *(old)*.
12. My sister drives *(carefully)* than I do, but I drive *(fast)* than she does. My brother drives the *(slowly)* of us all.
13. My brother gets up *(early)* than anybody in our family. That's because he starts work the *(early)* and has to travel the *(far)*.
14. I get *(much)* money than my brother but I spend *(little)* than he does. My sister has the *(little)* money because she's gone back to university to study for *(far)* qualifications.
15. I've travelled *(far)* around the world than anyone else in my family.
16. I speak German *(well)* than French, but my Arabic is *(bad)* than my French. Of course English is my *(good)* language.

BEAUCOUP / ENCORE + COMPARATIF ; **THAN** + PRONOM *(AZ 84, 85)*

***2. À partir des éléments fournis, construisez des phrases utilisant*** much / far / a lot ***ou*** even ***+ comparatif. Les symboles (+++, etc.) vous indiquent les degrés de comparaison.***

**Ex. :** nice: Sue (+++++); Joe (+)
*Sue is* ***much*** *nicer than Joe.*
**Ex. :** friendly: Ann (+++++); Sue (+++)
*Ann is* ***even*** *friendlier than Sue.*

1. intelligent: Joe (+++++); Alan (+)
2. easy: this question (+++++); the first question (+)
3. young: she (+++++); he (+)
4. drive fast: Mary (+++++); I (+)
5. fat: Bob (+++++); you (+)
6. sing well: you (+++++); she (+++)
7. work quickly: we (+++++); they (+++)

DOUBLES COMPARATIFS ; **THE** + COMPARATIF *(AZ 86, 87)*

***3. Complétez les phrases en utilisant des doubles comparatifs (DC) ou*** the ***+ comparatif (C).***

1. The weather is getting *(bad)*. (DC)
2. They are getting *(much)* complaints. (DC)
3. *(fat)* I get, *(happy)* I become. (C)
4. We listen to *(little)* modern music. (DC)
5. He was all *(pleased)* because it happened on his birthday. (C)
6. Everything is getting *(expensive)*. (DC)
7. *(little)* exercise we take, *(little)* energy we have. (C)
8. 'And Tony can play too.' 'So much *(good)*!' (C)
9. *(much)* she worries about it, *(little)* she sleeps. (C)
10. Skiing is becoming *(popular)*. (DC)

***Inventez quatre phrases en utilisant les tournures suivantes.***

I am getting *(de plus en plus)* …
… is/are getting *(de moins en moins)* …
The more …, the more …
The less …, the less …

SUPERLATIF ; COMPARATIF OU SUPERLATIF? *(AZ 88-90)*

**4. *Choisissez la forme qui convient. Parfois les deux formes sont possibles.***

1. It was *Ø/ the* cheapest car we could find.
2. Who played *Ø/ the* best?
3. Of all my photos this one is *Ø/ the* most interesting.
4. She can be *Ø/ the* most amusing when she's relaxed.
5. Your hair looks *Ø/ the* prettiest when it's short.
6. He's *Ø/ the* fastest 100 metres runner *of/ in* the world.
7. That's *Ø/ the* nicest thing anyone's ever said to me!
8. It was *Ø/ the* most violent crime *of/ in* the year!
9. Which of the two girls is the *more/ most* intelligent?
10. If only the *young/ younger* generation had more wisdom *(= sagesse)* and the *old/ older* generation had more energy!
11. The *stronger/ strongest* students usually take the exam after one year while the *weaker/ weakest* students take it the following year. The *better/ best* students often take it after only six months!

AS ... AS ; AS MUCH/ MANY ... AS *(AZ 44, 49)*

***5. Écrivez des phrases à l'aide de*** as ... as***, etc. Les symboles (+++, etc.) vous indiquent les degrés de comparaison.***

**Ex. :** tall: I (+++); she (+++)
*I'm **as tall as** her / she is.*

**Ex. :** clever: he (++); you (+++) *(not)*
*He isn't **as clever as** you / you are.*

**Ex. :** can swim fast: we (++++); they (++) *(twice)*
*We can swim **twice as fast as** them / they can.*

1. big: South America (++++); Europe (++) *(twice)*
2. speak French well : I (++); you (+++) *(not)*
3. interesting: London (+++); Paris (+++)
4. drink much beer: I (++); he (+++) *(not)*
5. (there) many people: China (+++++); the USA (+) *(five times)*
6. (there) much oil: Mexico (++); Saudi Arabia (+++) *(not)*

MOINS, LE MOINS *(AZ 83)*

***6. Complétez les phrases à l'aide des expressions proposées. Il y a parfois plusieurs possibilités.***

as   as few   as little   at least   fewer   fewest   least   less   than

1. 'My hotel was not ..... expensive ..... yours.' 'Yes, but yours was ..... comfortable ..... mine.'
2. I'm sorry to say this was the book we enjoyed .....
3. I try to eat ..... sugar as possible.
4. We've got ..... milk and ..... eggs ..... I thought we had.
5. We try to spend ..... days apart as possible.
6. It was the ..... interesting country she'd ever visited.
7. Who got the ..... points?
8. They've got ..... six dogs!
9. Sarah always spends the ..... money on holiday.
10. He's coming tomorrow – or ..... he said he was.

EXERCICE DE SYNTHÈSE *(AZ 80-90, 44, 49)*

***7. Traduisez en anglais.***

1. Il leur faut le plus possible d'argent.
2. C'est le bar le plus agréable *(= pleasant)* de la ville.
3. Voulez-vous nous adresser de plus amples renseignements *(= information)*? *(Please send us …)*
4. "Il a joué beaucoup plus mal que toi." "Tant mieux!"
5. Mon frère aîné est sur le point de se marier *(= get married).*
6. Il fait encore plus froid aujourd'hui qu'hier.
7. C'est le plus mauvais match de la saison *(= season).*
8. Elle devient de plus en plus faible *(= weak).*
9. Plus ils gagnent *(= earn)* d'argent, moins ils sont heureux.
10. Je suis d'autant plus désolé que je ne vous ai pas écrit.
11. C'est en janvier que le temps est le plus froid. *(The weather is …)*
12. Il ne danse pas aussi bien que vous.

# 10 *Be, have* et *do*

**BE** : FORMES *(AZ 59)*

***1. Mettez* be *à la forme qui convient. Utilisez des contractions lorsque c'est possible.***

1. '..... they ready?' 'No, not yet.'
2. Lucy and I ..... at home yesterday.
3. Of course he ..... at school today. It's Sunday!
4. Do ..... careful!
5. Please, ..*(not)*.. late!
6. I'm next, ..*(not)*.. I?
7. They feel he ..... very inflexible about this.
8. There's that car again. I think we ..... followed!
9. ..*(not)*.. she at the party last week?
10. Peter ..... very unlucky all his life.
11. If he had given us better directions, it ..... easy to find.

**BE ; HAVE** *(AZ 59, 61)*

***2. Mettez* be *ou* have *à la forme qui convient. Utilisez des contractions lorsque c'est possible.***

1. He ..... three dogs but no cats.
2. This car ..... over two metres wide.
3. She ..... woken up yet.
4. ..... you afraid when it happened?
5. 'Tea?' 'No, thanks. I ..... thirsty.'
6. ..... Anne and Tom arrived yet?
7. 'It's quite difficult.' 'Yes, you ..... right.'
8. Paul ..... gone outside.
9. Sue ..... 40, but she looks a lot younger.
10. Listen. I ..... an idea!
11. He ..... less than 50 kilos when he died.
12. 'What was that noise?' 'I think Sarah ..... fallen out of bed again!'

### HAVE (GOT) *(AZ 170)*

***3. Mettez* got *dans les phrases où il s'emploie fréquemment.***

1. We've three children.
2. I had a very nice teacher.
3. They haven't any money.
4. He often has his dog with him.
5. Have you the time, please?
6. She's red hair.
7. We have the pleasure of informing you that ...
8. I haven't a particular opinion on this matter.

### HAVE : ACTIVITÉS *(AZ 171)*

***4. Complétez les phrases avec les expressions ci-dessous et* have *à la forme qui convient.***

| | | | | |
|---|---|---|---|---|
| a cup of coffee | a look at | a nervous breakdown | | |
| a nice time | a rest | a shower | a swim | a terrible holiday |
| a try | a wonderful dream | lunch | | |

1. 'I ..... last night.' 'Really? What was it about?'
2. 'I can't do this.' 'Could I .....?'
3. 'We're going away for the weekend.' 'Well, .....!' 'Thanks, we will!'
4. 'Where's John?' 'In the bathroom. He ......'
5. '..*(you)*.. with Debby?' 'No, we weren't hungry, so we just ..... together.'
6. 'If you keep working like this, you .....!'
7. Come on. Let's ..... . The water looks lovely!
8. Can I ..... your CD collection?
9. You look really tired. Why ..*(not, you)*..?
10. We ..... last year. The plane was late. The hotel was awful. The food was horrible.

**DO** : INSISTANCE / CONTRASTE *(AZ 106)*

***5. Utilisez*** do ***à la forme qui convient pour marquer l'insistance ou le contraste, ou pour confirmer ce qui a été dit.***

1. She wants to meet you!
2. Stop doing that!
3. 'May I use your phone?' 'Yes.'
4. Generally speaking he's a vegetarian. But he eats fish.
5. 'You should tell her the truth.' 'I told her.'
6. 'They didn't finish the job.' 'They finished the job – two weeks ago.'
7. I thought she'd forget, and she forgot.
8. Well, as expected, he moved to London.

**DO** : REPRISE *(AZ 107)*

***6. Utilisez*** do, does ***ou*** did ***pour éviter les répétitions dans les phrases suivantes.***

1. 'Who wants to go by bus?' 'We want to go by bus.'
2. She stopped work the year before my dad stopped work.
3. Joe plays the piano and Sue plays the piano too.
4. You like chocolate more than I like chocolate.
5. 'Does Mr Smith live here?' 'Yes, he lives here.'
6. 'We had a great holiday.' 'We had a great holiday as well.'
7. 'I never sleep with the window open.' 'Really? I always sleep with the window open.'
8. We didn't start until Alison started.
9. I ski better than my sister skis.

**DO** ET **MAKE** *(AZ 108)*

***7. Répartissez les expressions ci-dessous entre*** do ***et*** make***.***

| |
|---|
| 100 kph   a big favour   a few sandwiches   a lot of harm<br>a terrible fuss   all the arrangements   an attempt<br>enquiries   her hair   her homework   her wedding dress<br>his duty   peace   some work   something stupid<br>the beds   the cleaning   too many mistakes<br>too much noise   your best |

*do*: 100 kph, ...   *make*: a few sandwiches, ...

# 11 Modaux : *can, could, may* et *might*

PERMISSION : **CAN, COULD, MAY, MIGHT, BE ALLOWED TO**
*(AZ 72, 74, 230, 231, 63)*
***1. Complétez les phrases suivantes. Il y a parfois plusieurs possibilités.***

1. Dad, ..... I have £10, please?
2. I'm sorry, sir, you ..... go in there: it .....
3. Waiter: ..... I have a clean glass, please?
4. ..... I see inside your bag, please, madam? *(formel)*
5. When I was a child I ..... to see horror films because my parents said they were too frightening.
6. You ..... all have something to eat here. The bus will leave again in an hour.
7. He asked me if he ..... use the phone.
8. Visitors ..... leave their bags and coats at reception.
9. This notice says we ..*(not)*.. to take photos in this museum.
10. Visiting ..*(not)*.. after ten o'clock in the evening.

CAPACITÉ : **CAN** ET **COULD** *(AZ 72, 73)*
***2. Cathy a maintenant six ans. Utilisez*** can / can't ***ou*** could / couldn't ***pour définir ses capacités à différents moments de son enfance.***
**Ex. :** three months old: cry (YES) / talk (NO)
*When she was three months old, she could cry but she couldn't talk.*

1. a year old: walk (YES) / run (NO)
2. two years old: use a knife and fork (YES) / dress herself (NO)
3. three years old: count from 1 to 10 (NO) / draw pictures (YES)
4. four years old: say the alphabet (YES) / write her name (YES)
5. five years old: read (YES) / tell the time (NO)
6. Now that she is six years old: programme the video (NO) / play with the computer (YES)

***Utilisez*** could / couldn't ***pour évoquer votre propre enfance en quatre phrases.***

CAPACITÉ, POSSIBILITÉ : **CAN, COULD, BE ABLE TO**

*(AZ 72, 73, 75, 62)*

***3. Choisissez la forme qui convient. Parfois les deux options sont possibles.***

1. I hope you *can/ could* come to my party on Friday.
2. She *can't/ isn't able to* be at university already: she looks too young!
3. We *can/ could* do it if we had more time.
4. They *can't/ couldn't* understand him when he spoke French.
5. You *can/ could* write to me from time to time!
6. I *can/ 'm able to* run five kilometres without stopping.
7. She'd love to *can/ be able to* swim well.
8. If you get this diploma you *could/ will be able to* work anywhere in the world.
9. He's never *could/ been able to* play tennis.
10. I like *can/ being able to* do what I want.
11. Unfortunately Ms Smith *cannot/ is unable to* see you today.

**COULD, WAS ABLE TO** ET **MANAGED TO** *(AZ 76)*

***4. Corrigez les phrases en remplaçant*** could ***par*** was able to ***ou*** managed to ***lorsque c'est nécessaire. (Il s'agit du passé.)***

1. He could find the keys after looking for them for nearly an hour.
2. When he was younger he could beat everyone at chess.
3. Finally I could get to sleep at three o'clock in the morning.
4. Tom could always sing better than his sister.
5. Everyone was very pleased because we could finish the job two days early.
6. She could swim when she was four.
7. The police could catch the criminals before they got away.

**MAY** ET **MIGHT** : POSSIBILITÉ, PROBABILITÉ *(AZ 230, 232)*

***5. Choisissez les formes correctes. Elles le sont parfois toutes les deux.***

1. She *may/ might* be in a meeting at the moment. I'm not sure.
2. They *may/ might* call us before the end of the week, but I don't think they will.
3. If he spoke more slowly, people *may/ might* understand him better.
4. Sorry, we don't have it here. You *may/ might* try the shop across the road.
5. Drive carefully when the roads are wet. If you don't, you *may/ might* have an accident.
6. He told me that he *may/ might* visit us in the spring.
7. You *may/ might* keep your voices down a little! We're trying to sleep!
8. If they worked harder they *may/ might* be more successful.
9. You *may/ might* ask Tom about this: he knows about cars.
10. I *may/ might* be wrong, but I think the sun is coming out at last!

**CAN, COULD, MAY** ET **MIGHT** + INFINITIF PASSÉ *(AZ 77, 233)*

***6. Complétez à l'aide de*** can, could, may ***ou*** might ***+ l'infinitif passé des verbes proposés. Il y a parfois plusieurs possibilités.***

1. He was very good-looking. He *(become)* a film star.
2. What *(happen)* to them? They *(not, disappear)*!
3. I was so angry with him that I *(kill)* him!
4. 'You *(tell)* me sooner!' 'But then you *(say)* something to Jill!'
5. 'OK, I *(be)* a bit stupid, but ...' 'A bit stupid? You *(start)* a fire! It *(be)* a disaster!'

EXERCICE DE SYNTHÈSE : PERMISSION, CAPACITÉ, POSSIBILITÉ

***7. Complétez à l'aide de*** can, could, may, might, be able to ***et*** manage to. ***Parfois plusieurs réponses sont possibles.***

1. ..... I speak to you privately, please, madame? *(AZ 74)*
2. ..... you close the door, please? *(AZ 73)*
3. Leave that alone. You ..... break it. *(AZ 232)*

4. We hope to ..... retire when we are 55. *(AZ 62)*
5. Please extinguish your cigarette, sir. Smoking ..... in this restaurant. *(AZ 63)*
6. 'Unfortunately I ..... speak Arabic.' 'Oh, Ali .....!' *(AZ 73)*
7. If he got more fresh air he ..... feel better. *(AZ 232)*
8. She ..... phone him after six o'clock. He's usually back by then. *(AZ 232)*
9. She ..... be a grandmother already – she's only 35! *(AZ 73)*
10. I ..... see anything because it was too dark. *(AZ 75)*
11. They said they ..... come, but I didn't think that they would. *(AZ 232)*
12. If I don't finish my homework quickly, Mum says I ..... watch the film. *(AZ 63, 73, 62)*
13. Although we didn't have a key we still ..... open the door. *(AZ 62)*
14. You ..... get up earlier in the morning!! *(AZ 73, 232)*
15. If I get this job we ..... pay all our debts. *(AZ 62)*

## 12 Modaux : *must, have to, need, should* et *ought*

**MUST** ET **HAVE (GOT) TO** *(AZ 244, 246)*

***1. Complétez avec*** must ***ou*** have (got) to ***à la forme qui convient.***

1. I'm becoming very fat: I really ..... take some exercise.
2. ..... she ..... wear glasses now?
3. I ..... talk to her last night.
4. You ..... visit us some time.
5. We ..*(not)*.. to take a taxi – Tom will drive us home.
6. With a big house like that they ..... be very rich.
7. He hopes he ..*(not)*.. move to London next year.
8. You ..*(not)*.. waste time.
9. I ..*(not)*.. talk to her since Tuesday.
10. It's not easy to ..... leave your family.
11. The dentist said you ..... brush your teeth more often.
12. If the weather is bad we ..... play the match later in the season.

**NEED** ET **NEEDN'T** *(AZ 248)*

***2. Choisissez la forme qui convient. Parfois les deux formes sont possibles.***

1. *Do you need/ Have you need of* more paper?
2. You need *buying/ to buy* the tickets in advance.
3. She needn't *wait/ to wait* for us.
4. We don't need *phoning/ to phone* her until tomorrow.
5. What do I need *saying/ to say* to them?
6. We *needn't/ don't need to* ask her permission.
7. He *doesn't need/ hasn't need of* us any more.
8. They needn't *come/ have come* so early. No one arrived until ten o'clock.
9. This house needs *painting/ to paint.*
10. We *needn't/ don't need to* hurry: there's lots of time.

**MUST HAVE** + PARTICIPE PASSÉ *(AZ 245)*

***3. Complétez à l'aide de*** must have / can't have ***+ participe passé ou*** had to***, en utilisant les verbes proposés.***

1. Here are Bob's keys: he *(forget)* them.
2. Jill *(go)* yet: her handbag is still here.
3. David left at four o'clock. He *(go)* to the dentist's.
4. He was in New York for only six hours. He *(see)* very much.
5. Because of the rain we *(stay)* inside most of the time.
6. You look really well! You *(have)* a good holiday.
7. There's nothing left in the fridge. They *(eat)* everything!
8. She didn't have enough money for a car, so she *(buy)* a motorbike.
9. I was so busy yesterday that I *(work)* until midnight.
10. With all that noise Pete and Sue *(get)* any sleep at all.
11. The documents aren't on Ann's desk. She *(take)* them home with her.

**SHOULD** (JE DEVRAIS, JE DOIS) ET **MUST** *(AZ 353, 357)*

***4. Transformez ces phrases en utilisant*** must ***ou*** should***.***

**Ex. :** It is very important for children to respect their parents.
*Children must respect their parents.*

**Ex. :** Possibly you need to relax a bit more.
*Possibly you should relax a bit more.*

1. It is vital for the nations of the world to learn to live together in peace.
2. Maybe we need to buy a bigger house.
3. It's very necessary for them to come today.
4. Perhaps it isn't a good idea for them to get married.
5. (The concert has been going on for over three hours.) It will probably be finished soon.
6. (His letter was sent two weeks ago.) It will certainly arrive this week.
7. (The job is nearly complete.) It's important for us not to stop now.
8. (I've done this kind of work before.) This job probably won't be very difficult.

**OUGHT** *(AZ 278)*

***5. Transformez les phrases suivantes en utilisant* ought.**

1. With your looks you should become an actor!
2. You shouldn't eat so many sweets!
3. Should I take that new job?
4. Paul should beat Don. He's a much better player.
5. She shouldn't take everything so seriously.
6. Should we clean the kitchen?

**SHOULD / OUGHT** + INFINITIF PASSÉ *(AZ 354, 279)*

***6. Construisez deux phrases pour chaque situation en utilisant* should *et* ought *+ infinitif passé. Utilisez des contractions lorsque c'est possible.***

**Ex. :** I felt very tired. *(go to bed early)*
*I should have gone to bed early.*
*I ought to have gone to bed early.*

1. I didn't have time to have breakfast. *(not get up late)*
2. The taxi to work was very expensive. *(catch the bus)*
3. I left some documents in the taxi. *(be more careful)*
4. He was very angry with me. *(remember our meeting)*
5. I got indigestion. *(not eat so much for lunch)*
6. I didn't finish the new brochure. *(work more quickly)*
7. My girlfriend was very angry with me. *(not forget to phone her)*
8. It was a terrible day! *(stay in bed)*

DEVOIR *(AZ 102)*

***7. Traduisez en anglais.***

1. Je ne dois pas perdre la clé.
2. Lorsque j'étais enfant, je devais me coucher à neuf heures.
3. On doit penser aux autres.
4. Ils devaient se marier *(= get married)*, mais ...
5. Tu devrais téléphoner à Paul.
6. Il devait devenir un écrivain célèbre *(= famous)*.
7. Je dois les voir demain.
8. S'ils quittaient Londres, elle devrait chercher un nouveau travail *(= job)*.
9. Onze heures : elle doit certainement être à son bureau maintenant.

DEVOIR *(AZ 102)*

***8. Traduisez en français les verbes en italique en utilisant le verbe "devoir".***

1. She *had to* travel to Paris every month.
2. He*'s supposed to* meet me at twelve.
3. They *mustn't* find out about this.
4. You *oughtn't to* worry about everything.
5. We *were to* buy a flat together.
6. The strong *ought to* help the weak.
7. I *was meeting* them outside the office.
8. We *have to* catch the eight o'clock train.
9. If they offered me the job I *would have to* accept it.
10. You *should* be more careful.
11. I *was supposed to* be the boss.
12. They *are to* discuss it again tomorrow.

EXERCICE DE SYNTHÈSE

***9. Complétez à l'aide de*** must, have (got) to, need, needn't, should, ought. ***Si plusieurs formes sont possibles, mettez-en au moins deux.***

1. British law says that children ..... stay at school until they are sixteen. *(AZ 244, 246)*
2. Perhaps he ..... inform the police. *(AZ 353, 278)*
3. If things don't get better we ..... sell the car. *(AZ 244, 246, 248)*
4. The doctor ..... come. I'm fine now. *(AZ 248)*
5. You've been travelling all day. You ..... be really tired. *(AZ 244)*
6. She doesn't want ..... leave her job. *(AZ 246)*
7. His shirt ..... washing. *(AZ 248)*
8. They ..... come quickly: it's life or death! *(AZ 244, 246)*
9. You ..... go in there. It might be dangerous. *(AZ 353, 278)*
10. I ..... see the dentist again tomorrow. I've made an appointment. *(AZ 248, 246)*
11. You ..... go by bus. A taxi is quicker. *(AZ 353, 278)*
12. I'm the boss: I ..... consult anybody! *(AZ 246, 248)*

EXERCICE DE SYNTHÈSE : **MUST / SHOULD / OUGHT TO** + INFINITIF PASSÉ *(AZ 245, 354, 279)*

***10. Complétez les phrases suivantes à l'aide du modal qui convient, suivi du verbe entre parenthèses à l'infinitif passé.***

1. You ..... *(remember)* her name. She was very angry with you.
2. 'Your bedroom window is still open.' 'Really? I ..... *(forget)* to close it.'
3. It was a mistake: I ..... *(tell)* her anything.
4. Where are my keys? I ..... *(leave)* them in my office.
5. You ..... *(write)* to me! I was very worried about you!

# 13 La modalité: autres usages

**HAD BETTER** *(AZ 164)*

***1. Donnez quelques conseils pratiques en utilisant*** had better (not) ***et les expressions ci-dessous.***

**Ex. :** I feel ill. *You'd better not go to work.*

| | | | | |
|---|---|---|---|---|
| call the police | clean them | eat it | forget it | go to work |
| have a haircut | light a cigarette | play football | | |
| take an aspirin | take some exercise | wake her up | | |

1. My head hurts.
2. The baby's asleep at last.
3. There's been an accident.
4. I'm putting petrol in my car.
5. My hair's too long.
6. The food in the fridge doesn't smell very nice.
7. My shoes are very dirty.
8. I've got an important appointment today.
9. I'm getting fat.
10. My leg hurts.

**BE SUPPOSED TO** *(AZ 65)*

***2. Complétez les phrases à l'aide de*** be supposed to ***à la forme qui convient (affirmative ou négative) et des expressions ci-dessous.***

**Ex. :** Give it back to me! You*'re not supposed to touch my things!*

| | | |
|---|---|---|
| be in Cambridge at five o'clock | be very charming | |
| come by plane | eat meat | get them from Ann |
| meet him | play the match | smoke in here |
| touch my things | wear these on your head | |

1. 4.30! I must hurry! I .....
2. I think you'll like her. She .....
3. I ..... at the station, but I forgot!
4. She's vegetarian, so she .....
5. 'Who's got the keys?' 'I thought you .....'

6. Please extinguish your cigarette, madame. You .....
7. He ..... but there was a problem at the airport.
8. You ..... not on your feet!
9. They ..... on Saturday, but the weather was very bad.

**USED TO** ET **WOULD** *(AZ 393, 394)*

***3. Complétez chaque phrase avec*** used to***. Mettez aussi*** would ***lorsqu'il est possible.***

1. We ..... see each other at school everyday.
2. She ..... have a lot of friends.
3. I ..*(not)*.. live in such a big house.
4. My father ..... work down a coal mine.
5. We ..... go skiing every February.
6. I ..*(sometimes)*.. climb trees when I was young.
7. This ..... be a church.
8. ..*(he)*.. live in Ireland?
9. They ..*(often)*.. go to the theatre together.
10. We ..*(not)*.. like them very much.
11. My grandmother ..... have beautiful hair.

**WILL** ET **WOULD** (SENS FRÉQUENTATIF) *(AZ 409)*

***4. Récrivez les phrases en utilisant*** will ***ou*** would ***et les mots proposés.***

**Ex. :** I start work at six o'clock in the morning. *(often)*
*I will often start work at six o'clock in the morning.*

1. My husband bought me flowers. *(sometimes)*
2. Many animals don't come out until after dark. *(usually)*
3. We went out for lunch. *(occasionally)*
4. I don't drink if I'm driving. *(ever)*
5. When I was a little boy I walked to school. *(always)*
6. Cats don't play with dogs. *(generally)*
7. He didn't speak unless he was spoken to. *(usually)*
8. A rhinoceros runs faster than a horse. *(normally)*

**WOULD RATHER** *(AZ 414)*

***5. Transformez les phrases à l'aide de*** would rather***.***

1. 'Shall we go?' 'I'd prefer to stay a little longer.'
2. They'd prefer to die rather than abandon their country.

→

3. Would you prefer to play with me or with Tom?
4. I hear you'd prefer not to discuss the matter.
5. 'Smell this!' 'I'd prefer not to.'
6. We'd prefer you to leave us alone.
7. I'd prefer the government to spend more on education.
8. We'd prefer them not to make so much noise.
9. Her parents would prefer her to study harder.
10. 'Is it OK if we smoke?' 'We'd prefer you not to.'

***Complétez les phrases suivantes en exprimant votre point de vue.***

I'd rather ... than ...
I'd rather my friends ...
I'd rather the government ...

## 14 L'infinitif

INFINITIF AVEC OU SANS **TO** *(AZ 193, 194)*

***1. Mettez*** to ***là où il est nécessaire.***

1. He doesn't know what do.
2. Would they rather go or stay?
3. We've no wish make trouble.
4. You should be more careful.
5. It's too late start now.
6. It's stupid not ask for help.
7. We might not have time tomorrow.
8. I think you'd better take a taxi.
9. 'Do you want come with us?' 'No, thanks. We prefer walk.'
10. Why not buy my car?
11. Let me see that!
12. What are you trying do with it?
13. We were disappointed not see him.
14. I didn't hear you come in last night.
15. He isn't experienced enough do it.
16. We're beginning understand her.
17. I hope never talk to her again.
18. We'll do anything except look after your children.
19. He would like invite you to dinner.
20. My cat never does anything but sleep.

INFINITIFS PASSÉ, PASSIF ET PROGRESSIF *(AZ 195)*

***2. Mettez les verbes entre parenthèses à la forme de l'infinitif qui convient (passé, passif ou progressif).***

**Ex. :** She just wants *to be respected* a little more. *(respect)*

1. He seems ..... a lot more these days. *(smoke)*
2. Your office will need ..... very soon. *(repaint)*
3. We were happy ..... the town when we did. *(leave)*
4. I hope ..... New York in May. *(visit)*
5. These presents are ..... before Christmas. *(not open)*
6. They were disappointed ..... their exams last year. *(not pass)*
7. We would like ..... abroad by the end of the year. *(live)*
8. You could ..... the train yesterday. *(take)*
9. This wine should ..... for at least five years. *(not drink)*

**TO, IN ORDER TO, SO AS TO** + INFINITIF *(AZ 196)*

***3. Reliez les deux phrases proposées ...***

***A : à l'aide de*** to ***+ infinitif.***

1. She went into the shop. She wanted to buy a newspaper.
2. Could I use your bathroom? I'd like to wash my hands.
3. He went to the optician. He wanted to get some new glasses.
4. Could you phone my husband? Tell him I'll be late.

***B : à l'aide de*** in order (not) to***, et*** so as (not) to ***+ infinitif.***

5. We wrote to them. We wanted to invite them to our party.
6. He didn't tell her the truth. He didn't want to worry her.
7. Let's do it now. We don't want to waste time tomorrow.
8. I'm doing an evening class. I want to learn Spanish.
9. They were speaking very quietly. They didn't want to let me hear their conversation.
10. I always work very carefully. I don't want to make mistakes.
11. She leaves the house very early. She wants to miss the traffic.
12. He cut off his moustache. He didn't want to be recognised.

PROPOSITION INFINITIVE ; **FOR ... TO ...** *(AZ 197, 143)*

***4. Construisez les phrases en utilisant une proposition infinitive.***

**A**

1. We'd like / they / meet John.
2. He didn't want / she / hear about it.
3. Would you prefer / they / speak French?
4. I want / everyone / know / I love you!
5. They don't like / we / use the phone.
6. She would prefer / I / not come back.
7. He hates / the children / be impolite.
8. We need / they / pay us the money.
9. Order / he / get the car!

**B**

10. It's essential / he / try to relax.
11. It still isn't clear enough / we / see anything.
12. Wait / the bus / stop.
13. We arranged / she / come on Monday.
14. I can't find anything / they / wear.
15. The piano is / Tom / practise on.

INFINITIF : REPRISE PAR **TO** *(AZ 198)*

***5. Complétez ces dialogues à l'aide des verbes proposés.***

**Ex. :** 'Did you ring Nick?' 'I *tried to*, but his phone was engaged.' *(try)*

1. 'Are you going to go to university?' 'I ....., but it depends on my exam results.' *(hope)*
2. 'Did you agree to work on Sunday.' 'No, I ..... . I can't work everyday!' *(refuse)*
3. 'Would you like to come for a walk with us?' 'Oh, yes, I ..... . I'll get my coat.' *(love)*
4. 'Did you remember to get a newspaper?' 'No, I ..... . Sorry!' *(forget)*
5. 'May I have some more soup, please?' 'Sure. Have as much as you ..... . There's lots!' *(like)*

EXERCICE DE SYNTHÈSE : INFINITIFS *(AZ 193-198, 143)*

***6. Corrigez les phrases suivantes.***

1. They didn't know how open it.
2. Could you to help us, please?
3. We were happy to be arrived on time.
4. He's gone out for post a letter.
5. We want that she has a good education.
6. I prefer spend weekends on my own.
7. You'd better to hurry up.
8. He promised to never tell anybody.
9. Why not to join us?
10. I'll wait that he call us on Monday.
11. Do what you like to. I don't care.
12. It's impossible forget her face.
13. Look what you made me to do!
14. It's too complicated for that we understand.
15. I don't want to do anything but to relax.
16. Take your shoes off for not to dirty the carpet.
17. Have you got anything them to play with?

# 15 *-ed* et *-ing*

**-ED** ET **-ING** *(AZ 115)*

***1. Complétez les phrases suivantes en utilisant les verbes ci-dessous à la forme qui convient (*-ed *ou* -ing*).***

annoy bore destroy excite fascinate frighten
interest shock translate

1. This book is really ..... I can't stop reading it.
2. Calm down: don't get so .....!
3. At the moment he's ..... a book into Chinese.
4. I wish he'd stop singing all the time. It's very .....!
5. We were all ..... when we received the news of her terrible car accident.
6. They're .....: they say they've got nothing to do.
7. I'm very ..... in astronomy. I've got lots of books on it.
8. That video was so ..... that we slept badly afterwards. →

9. Millions of trees are ..... every year.
10. Let's watch something else: this isn't very ....., is it?

ÊTRE + PARTICIPE PASSÉ *(AZ 127)*

***2. Traduisez en anglais.***

1. Le match est terminé *(= finish).*
2. La voiture avait été volée.
3. J'étais couché sur mon lit.
4. Pourquoi es-tu assis comme ça?
5. Ma mère est déjà arrivée.
6. "Où est Christine?" "Elle est partie."
7. "Quand est-ce que vous êtes partis?" "Lundi."
8. "Tu es déjà *(= ever)* sortie avec lui?" "Non." (present perfect)
9. Il est resté *(= stay)* au lit toute la journée *(= all day).* (present perfect)

**-ING** : SUJET/ ATTRIBUT DU SUJET/ COMPLÉMENT ; **IT ... -ING ; WORTH** (+ **-ING**) *(AZ 199, 200, 413)*

***3. Complétez les phrases suivantes en utilisant les verbes ci-dessous à la forme en* -ing*.***

| |
|---|
| buy clean laugh interrupt repair say shout ski spend surf tell travel |

1. I really enjoyed ..... until I broke both my legs last year.
2. ..... by bus can be quite tiring.
3. They left without ..... where they were going.
4. It's worth ..... at least a week in Venice. There's so much to see.
5. The job I like least is ..... the bathroom.
6. He wants to start ..... next year, but first he's got to learn to swim!
7. It's not worth ..... the books. You can use mine.
8. Excuse me ..... you, but could you repeat the question, please?
9. Stop all this ..... immediately!! There's too much noise.
10. It isn't worth ..... it. It would cost too much!
11. He's quite sensitive. He hates us ..... at him.
12. It's no use ..... me your problems. I don't work here.

**-ING** APRÈS LES PRÉPOSITIONS ; **TO + -ING ; LOOK FORWARD TO ; BE USED TO** *(AZ 202, 203, 226, 395)*

***4. Construisez des phrases vraisemblables en utilisant les éléments fournis.***

| | | |
|---|---|---|
| 1. I'm looking forward | about | getting up early. |
| 2. I sometimes walk to work | | being forty. |
| 3. I'm used | after | having to pay for the royal family. |
| 4. I often talk | | keeping it in the bank. |
| 5. I object | before | finishing a good book. |
| 6. I'm fed up | | knowing why. |
| 7. I prefer spending money | instead of | not eating meat. |
| 8. I always listen to the radio | | trying to look younger than I am. |
| 9. I'm not looking forward | to | driving. |
| 10. I often feel really happy | with | eating less. |
| 11. I'll never get used | | visiting Japan next summer. |
| 12. I always feel a little sad | without | going to sleep. |

APRÈS AVOIR VU = **AFTER SEEING, ...** *(AZ 204)*

***5. Récrivez les phrases en utilisant*** after, before ***ou*** without **+** -ing.

**Ex. :** They left the party. They hadn't said goodbye.
*They left the party without saying goodbye.*

1. After he finished the housework, he switched on the TV.
2. I don't like to criticise a film before I have seen it.
3. She took the car. She didn't ask my permission.
4. I read the book after I had seen the film.
5. Before we saw these examples of her work, we didn't think she was a very good painter.
6. They got married after they had known each other for only a week.
7. He left the restaurant before he had his coffee.
8. You said that. You didn't move your lips!

**-ING** : FORME PROGRESSIVE ABRÉGÉE *(AZ 205)*

***6. Récrivez les phrases suivantes en utilisant une forme progressive abrégée.***

**Ex. :** Who's that woman? She's speaking to Tom.
*Who's that woman speaking to Tom?*

1. The man who is walking towards us is Anne's husband.
2. Did you hear the baby? He was crying.
3. The police caught her. She was driving too fast on the motorway.
4. Behind our house there's a little road. It goes down to the river.
5. Can you smell something? It's burning.
6. I love to hear birds which are singing.
7. The classroom was full of children who were smiling happily.

EXERCICE DE SYNTHÈSE : PARTICIPES, **-ING**

***7. Corrigez les erreurs dans les phrases suivantes. (Attention : certaines sont tout à fait correctes.)***

1. I'm not interesting in computer games. *(AZ 115)*
2. To ski is not as easy as it looks. *(AZ 199)*
3. He's always talking about leaving his job. *(AZ 202)*
4. Is this idea worth to consider? *(AZ 413)*
5. It's no use to pretend you are sick. *(AZ 200)*
6. She's looking forward to getting married. *(AZ 203, 226)*
7. We're not used to speak French. *(AZ 203, 395)*
8. I didn't want to say anything before to have talked to my wife. *(AZ 204)*
9. We heard the sound of glass which was breaking. *(AZ 205)*

# 16 Infinitif ou *-ing*

**LIKE** ET **WOULD LIKE** *(AZ 220)*

***1. Complétez le dialogue en utilisant les éléments ci-dessous. Mettez les verbes entre parenthèses à la forme qui convient (*to*-infinitif ou* -ing*). Il peut y avoir plusieurs possibilités.***

| | | | |
|---|---|---|---|
| Do you like | doesn't like | Don't you like | I don't like |
| I like | I'd like | Would you like | would you like |

A: What ..1.. *(drink)*?
B: ..2.. a coffee, please.
A: ..3.. decaffeinated?
B: Yes, I prefer it.
A: ..4.. *(have)* it in here or outside on the balcony?
B: In here please. ..5.. *(sit)* in the sun.
A: ..6.. *(get)* sun-tanned?
B: No, ..7.. *(stay)* out of the sun. Unfortunately my body ..8.. the sun.

**-ING** APRÈS CERTAINS VERBES *(AZ 201)*

***2. Mettez l'infinitif ou la forme en* -ing*. Si les deux formes sont possibles, mettez-les toutes les deux.***

1. Would you consider *(look)* for a new job?
2. We continue *(work)* until midnight.
3. Let's avoid *(discuss)* politics.
4. Would you prefer *(talk)* in private?
5. Do you want to go on *(watch)* this or shall I turn it off?
6. I keep on *(forget)* her name.
7. She couldn't bear *(leave)* him.
8. He can't stand *(waste)* time.
9. We'd love *(visit)* you next year.
10. As soon as the music started everyone began *(dance)*.
11. They suggested *(try)* one more time.
12. I hate not *(finish)* things.
13. He's spent a lot of time *(think)* about what to do next.
14. She left her job in London and she went on *(work)* in the family business.

→

15. We can't help *(miss)* our daughter now that she's in New Zealand.
16. I wouldn't like *(meet)* him on a dark night!

INFINITIF OU **-ING : AFRAID, REMEMBER** ET **FORGET, SEE** ET **HEAR, STOP, TRY** *(AZ 15, 344, 350, 370, 391)*

***3. Complétez ces phrases avec les verbes ci-dessous à la forme qui convient : infinitif avec ou sans*** to, -ing ***avec ou sans préposition. Quand les deux formes sont possibles, mettez-les toutes les deux.***

| | | | | | | | | |
|---|---|---|---|---|---|---|---|---|
| ask | call | close | eat | find | forget | get | give | go |
| laugh | meet | pay | play | put | read | talk | | |

1. He was always afraid ..... something.
2. I've always been afraid ..... my poems in public.
3. Did you remember ..... the gardener? I think it was £30.
4. I'll never forget him ..... me to marry him.
5. Do you remember ..... him at the party? He was the one with the funny glasses.
6. Could you lend me some money, please? I forgot ..... to the bank today.
7. 'Did you see her ..... with the children?' 'Yes. They seemed to be enjoying themselves.'
8. They know our secret: they heard us ..... last night.
9. I heard her ..... the order to shoot him.
10. We saw him ..... the key in his pocket.
11. They stopped ..... petrol just outside Bordeaux.
12. Please stop ..... those sweets! It's nearly lunch time.
13. It was so funny that I couldn't stop myself .....
14. They tried ..... the house but without success.
15. Have you tried ..... the police?

### *4. Choisissez les formes correctes.*

1. Do you find *drawing / to draw* easier than *painting / to paint*? *(AZ 199)*
2. When she had told me about Tom, she went on *telling / to tell* me about Paul. *(AZ 201)*
3. It isn't worth *keeping / to keep* it any longer. *(AZ 413)*
4. Don't forget *sending / to send* a postcard. *(AZ 344)*
5. He died without *regaining / to have regained* consciousness. *(AZ 204)*
6. Why do you object to me *calling / call* you by your first name? *(AZ 199)*
7. We would hate *missing / to miss* the match. *(AZ 201)*
8. Do you mind *working / to work* outside? *(AZ 201)*
9. Did you remember *turning / to turn* the lights off? *(AZ 344)*
10. Have you got used to *travelling / travel* to London every day? *(AZ 395)*
11. Thank you *for being / to have been* so good to the children. *(AZ 204)*
12. We saw them *waiting / to wait* at the busstop for more than half an hour. *(AZ 205, 350)*
13. Would you like *coming / to come* with us? *(AZ 220)*
14. I remember *hearing / to hear* this as a child. *(AZ 344)*
15. It hasn't stopped *raining / to rain* all day. *(AZ 370)*
16. Try *turning / to turn* the handle the other way. That might work. *(AZ 391)*
17. I've been trying *speaking / to speak* to you since Tuesday. *(AZ 391)*
18. How can we stop it *happening / happen* again? *(AZ 370)*
19. I couldn't imagine *living / to live* like that. *(AZ 201)*

# 17 Les temps des verbes : présent

PRÉSENT SIMPLE *(AZ 307, 308)*

***1. Transformez les phrases suivantes en utilisant les indications fournies entre parenthèses.***
***(A) = affirmation ; (Q) = question ; (N) = négation.***

**Ex. :** I work here. (**Q** *she*) *Does she work here?*

1. She doesn't play computer games. (**A** *he*)
2. Do they worry a lot? (**N** *you*)
3. You don't usually try hard in English lessons. (**A** *she*)
4. We hope to go to university next year. (**Q** *Why, they*)
5. I brush my teeth after eating. (**N** *he*)
6. Do you go to the theatre? (**A** *I*)
7. The plane doesn't leave until 10.00. (**Q** *When, train*)
8. They miss Tom and Ann. (**N** *we*)
9. We go to church on Sunday. (**Q** *he*)
10. Does he study music? (**N** *they*)

PRÉSENT PROGRESSIF *(AZ 309, 310)*

***2. Mettez les verbes au présent progressif. Utilisez des contractions lorsque c'est possible.***

**Crisis on Mars!**

Mars Probe 7: 'Hello, Mission Control. This is Mars Probe 7. Astronaut Ruskov (1) *open* the door of the spacecraft. She (2) *climb* down onto the surface. She (3) *move* very slowly.'

Mission Control: 'Ruskov, this is Mission Control. How (4) *you feel* ?'

Ruskov: 'I (5) *feel* fine. I (6) *examine* some rocks. Now I (7) *walk* away from the spacecraft in the direction of a small crater.'

MC: '(8) *your instruments function* all right? We (9) *not get* very clear signals.'

R: 'I (10) *look at* the transmitter now. ... Something is wrong. I (11) *go back* to the spacecraft.'

MC: 'Ruskov, Your signals (12) *become* very unclear.'

R: 'Mission Control, can you hear me? Radiation levels (13) *go up*. My respirator (14) *not function* correctly … My God! What's that? Something (15) *approach* me from the crater! It (16) *hold* a … Aaaaaaaaaaaaaaaaargh!'

MC: 'Ruskov, Ruskov, can you hear me? Can you hear me? What (17) *happen*? …'

EXERCICE DE SYNTHÈSE : PRÉSENT SIMPLE OU PRÉSENT PROGRESSIF ? *(AZ 311)*

***3. Mettez le verbe à la forme qui convient. Il peut y avoir deux possibilités.***

**Old friends**

Ann: Betty, it's lovely to see you again – after such a long time!

Betty: Yes, I know! … So tell me, Ann: how (1) *things go* at the moment?

A: Oh, OK, thanks. You know, I (2) *work* for an international bank these days …

B: Really? Interesting! … Hey, but what's that sound?

A: Oh, that's Paul. He (3) *play* his violin up in his bedroom.

B: Hey, that's marvellous. (4) *he practise* a lot?

A: Yes, every evening. He sometimes (5) *give* concerts at school! … But listen – how is Quebec: (6) *you like* living there?

B: Yes, it's great, but it (7) *snow* a lot, and I still (8) *miss* England.

A: (9) *you ski*?

B: Yes, frequently. Pierre and the children (10) *ski* very well, but I'm not very good. But I (11) *enjoy* it all the same.

A: And what (12) *you work* on at the moment? A new novel?

B: Yes, I (13) *write* something about the North American Indians.

A: Fascinating. … And (14) *you speak* French now?

B: Oui, pas mal! But most people (15) *speak* English too, so it's never a problem.

A: Oh dear … I (16) *travel* to Paris every month on business, so I (17) *need* to make some progress in my French!

B: It's just a question of time … But tell me. What about your love life?

A: Mm, well (18) *you remember* Patrick Johnson? …

COMPARAISON DES DEUX TEMPS PRÉSENTS *(AZ 311)*

***4. Écrivez six phrases vous concernant en utilisant l'un des temps présents et les mots ci-dessous.***

1. every morning
2. tomorrow evening
3. often
4. at the moment
5. when I have time
6. on Saturday

VERBES SANS FORMES PROGRESSIVES *(AZ 399)*

***5. Parmi les phrases suivantes, corrigez celles où la forme progressive ne convient pas.***

1. She's having a baby in March.
2. Leave her alone: she's thinking.
3. Right now he is doubting everything you tell him.
4. When is he seeing the doctor?
5. We're being followed.
6. You are being very stupid.
7. I'm not seeing why we have to do it.
8. How are you feeling today?
9. Who are you thinking you are?

**ALWAYS** ET LES TEMPS PROGRESSIFS *(AZ 28)*

***6. Des attitudes ou des habitudes vous gênent chez vous-même ou chez les autres. Utilisez les expressions ci-dessous avec*** always ***et le présent progressif pour construire cinq phrases qui reflètent vos observations.***

**Ex. :** *I'm always forgetting people's names.*
*My boss is always losing her glasses.*

| |
|---|
| ask stupid questions   break things   cause trouble<br>complain   criticise other people   do stupid things<br>forget names/ keys/ glasses/ etc.   get angry<br>laugh at people   lose keys/ glasses / etc.<br>make cruel remarks   make mistakes<br>talk about himself/ herself   talk about other people behind their backs   tell lies   use bad language |

PRÉTÉRIT SIMPLE ET PARTICIPE PASSÉ (VERBES IRRÉGULIERS) *(AZ 316, 397)*

***1. Donnez le prétérit et le participe passé de ces verbes.***

build choose come fall feel go hide leave make pay run sell send show steal teach think throw wake write

*Prétérit : ...* *Participe passé : ...*

PRÉTÉRIT PROGRESSIF (ET PRÉTÉRIT SIMPLE) *(AZ 318)*

***2. Choisissez entre le prétérit simple et progressif.***

'Well, I (1) *took/ was taking* my little boy to school when I (2) *saw/ was seeing* a man run out of the bank. He (3) *wore/ was wearing* a mask and he (4) *carried/ was carrying* a gun. As he (5) *got/ was getting* into a car in front of the bank, a woman (6) *ran/ was running* out of the bank and (7) *shouted/ was shouting* for help. The alarm in the bank (8) *rang/ was ringing* now and everyone (9) *looked/ was looking* to see what (10) *happened/ was happening.* I (11) *went/ was going* to help the woman – she (12) *cried/ was crying.* Then the police (13) *arrived/ were arriving.*'

PRESENT PERFECT SIMPLE ET PRÉTÉRIT SIMPLE *(AZ 312, 313, 316, 317)*

***3. Récrivez les phrases en utilisant les mots entre parenthèses. Faites attention aux temps (présent perfect simple ou prétérit simple).***

**Ex. :** Did you hear Mozart's 'Requiem'? *(ever)*
*Have you ever heard Mozart's 'Requiem'?*

1. He's left the company. *(last May)*
2. We visited Ireland. *(already)*
3. Your father died. *(I'm very sorry to tell you ...)*
4. War has broken out. *(in 1939)*
5. My parents moved to London. *(not yet)*
6. I saw him at the golf club. *(never)*
7. Did they finish their homework? *(yet)*

→

8. His sister has worked in Germany. *(When ...)*
9. We haven't met her husband. *(at Sarah's dinner party)*
10. I lost my key. *(I can't open the door because ...)*
11. He has had a lot of girlfriends. *(... when he was at university)*

**FOR, SINCE** ET **AGO** *(AZ 100, 18)*

***4. Transformez les phrases suivantes en utilisant*** for, since ***ou*** ago***. Attention aux temps (present perfect simple et prétérit simple).***
***(Dans cet exercice on est mardi 21 juin 1994.)***

**Ex. :** I haven't seen her since March. *(ago)*
*I saw her three months ago.*

1. They've worked for this company for five years. *(since)*
2. You haven't talked to her since Sunday. *(for)*
3. She hasn't visited her mother for three weeks. *(ago)*
4. He wrote to me two months ago. *(since)*
5. I've known him since 1974. *(for)*
6. We had a world war 49 years ago. *(since)*
7. You haven't cooked dinner for five days. *(ago)*
8. We haven't been to the cinema since Christmas. *(for)*

PRESENT PERFECT PROGRESSIF ; **FOR** ET **SINCE** *(AZ 314, 100)*

***5. Écrivez une phrase correspondant à chaque situation à l'aide du present perfect et de*** for ***ou*** since***, s'il y a lieu.***

**Ex. :** The ground is wet. There are rain clouds in the sky.
*It has been raining.*

1. It started snowing two hours ago. It's still snowing.
2. She is holding a tennis racket. She looks hot and tired.
3. The baby started crying at three o'clock this morning. The baby is still crying.
4. I had my first Spanish class a month ago. I'm still learning Spanish.
5. Bob is drying his hands in the kitchen. The washing-up looks nice and clean.
6. Sarah moved to Marseilles in March. She's still living there.
7. My father is closing the newspaper and putting it down on the table.

PRESENT PERFECT PROGRESSIF (OU SIMPLE) *(AZ 314)*

***6. Corrigez les verbes en italique en utilisant le present perfect progressif ou simple.***

1. They *are looking* for a bigger flat for a long time.
2. He *isn't feeling* very well since his mother died.
3. Have a cup of tea – you look tired. *Did* you *work* hard?
4. I*'m trying* to talk to her since Monday.
5. How long *are* they *working* for this company?
6. We *are* here since four o'clock.
7. Look at you. Your clothes are really dirty! *Did* you *play* in the mud *(= boue)* again? I told you not to!
8. He *knows* about it for a long time.

PLUPERFECT *(AZ 295, 296)*

***7. Voici quel a été l'emploi du temps de Mary samedi dernier. Faites le point sur ses activités à différents moments de la journée, en utilisant le pluperfect simple ou progressif.***

**Ex. :** 7.30 am: lie in the bath / for

*She had been lying in the bath for half an hour.*

| | |
|---|---|
| **7.00 – 7.45:** | in the bath |
| **8.15 – 8.45:** | breakfast |
| **9.00 – 10.00:** | read the newspaper |
| **10.30 – 11.30:** | make her phonecalls |
| **12.00 – 1.00:** | write her letters |
| **1.00 – 2.30:** | lunch |
| **3.00 – 6.00:** | in town |
| **7.15 – 8.30:** | get dressed |
| **9.00 – 11.00:** | dinner |
| **12.00 – 9.00:** | bed |

1. 8.45 am: just finish
2. 9.15 am: read / since
3. 10.30 am: not start … yet
4. 12.00 pm: just begin
5. 1.45 pm: have lunch / since
6. 5.00 pm: be in town / for
7. 8.30 pm: just get dressed
8. 10.00 pm: eat / since
9. 4.00 am: be asleep / for

EXERCICE DE SYNTHÈSE *(AZ 312-314, 316-318, 295, 296)*

***8. Complétez les phrases suivantes en choisissant la forme verbale qui convient (prétérit, present perfect ou pluperfect, simple ou progressif). Utilisez des contractions lorsque c'est possible.***

1. '*(you, wait)* for a long time?' 'I *(stand)* here since 12 o'clock.' 'But I thought we *(agree)* to meet at 1 o'clock!' 'I *(say)* 12 o'clock, but you *(not listen)*, as usual! You *(do)* the same thing to me last week too! Well, I *(have)* enough of this treatment! Goodbye!!!'
2. 'And what *(the man, wear)*?' 'Well, it *(rain)*, so I *(can not)* see very clearly.' 'What *(he, do)* when you first *(see)* him?' 'He *(try)* to open the kitchen window. He *(use)* some kind of metal bar.' 'Where *(you, stand)* at the time?' 'At the bedroom window. I *(put)* some flowers in a vase.' '*(you, hear)* anything?' 'No, I *(listen)* to the radio.'
3. 'How long *(she, be)* with the bank?' 'Well, she *(join)* us five years ago and she *(work)* in this branch for the last two years.' 'When she *(come)* here, *(she, do)* work like this before?' 'Yes, at her last bank, but she told me she *(not enjoy)* it there.' '*(she, have)* any problems since she *(arrive)* here?' 'No. She *(work)* very well.'

# 19 Les temps des verbes : futur

FUTUR ET CONDITIONNEL *(AZ 149, 91)*

***1. Complétez les phrases suivantes par*** will / won't ***ou*** would / wouldn't. ***Utilisez des contractions lorsque c'est possible.***

1. Where ..... we go after the match tomorrow?
2. I ..... do that if I were you. It's too dangerous!
3. OK, I ..... see you on Wednesday. Bye!
4. What ..... he do if she left him?
5. If the weather is good we ..... go for a walk.
6. If you miss the six o'clock train you ..... arrive until after midnight.
7. I ..... love to see you again.
8. I promise we ..... touch anything.

**GOING TO** *(AZ 150)*

***2. Construisez des phrases en utilisant*** be going to ***et les mots fournis.***

**Ex. :** I / visit my parents / next weekend.
*I'm going to visit my parents next weekend.*

1. I think / it / rain / this afternoon.
2. I / pass / my driving test / before my next birthday.
3. I / stop / smoking / before the end of this year.
4. I / get / a better job / one of these days.
5. I / not get married / again.
6. I / never be / rich.
7. I hope / the government / not put up / taxes *(= impôts)*.
8. I hope / there not be / a nuclear disaster / before the year 2000.

***Modifiez quatre des phrases ci-dessus de manière à ce qu'elles expriment votre pensée.***

FUTUR : PRÉSENT PROGRESSIF ET PRÉSENT SIMPLE *(AZ 151)*

***3. Mettez le verbe entre parenthèses à la forme qui convient du présent simple ou progressif. Utilisez des contractions lorsque c'est possible.***

1. I ..... golf next Saturday. *(play)*
2. The 5.45 train from Lyons ..... at 8.15. *(arrive)*
3. We ..... the house at about two o'clock. *(leave)*
4. ..... you ..... to the party on Friday? *(come)*
5. I'm sorry. I ..... a guitar lesson this evening. *(have)*
6. She ..... me at ten o'clock. *(phone)*
7. Why ..... you ..... to Paris in March? *(go)*
8. What time ..... your plane .....? *(take off)*
9. When ..... she ..... John tonight? *(meet)*

**WILL, SHALL** ET LE PRÉSENT *(AZ 152, 352, 151)*

***4. Corrigez les formes verbales erronées. Utilisez des contractions lorsque c'est possible.***

1. If you make any more trouble, they call the police.
2. I tell you everything later.
3. The train for Marseilles leaves at 9.12.
4. If Tom doesn't hurry up, we go without him.
5. Shall you make me a sandwich, please?
6. 'Is that the phone?' 'It's all right – I get it.'
7. Don't worry. My mum shall help you.
8. 'Do we take a taxi?' 'Yes, good idea.'
9. Coffee for us, and the children will have some lemonade, please.
10. I give it to you on Monday. OK?

**WILL** ET **WOULD** *(AZ 410)*

***5. Complétez les phrases suivantes avec*** will ***ou*** would***. Parfois les deux formes sont possibles.***

1. ..... you wait outside, please?
2. 'Can someone meet Ann at the station?' 'We .....'
3. Please ..... you turn the lights off when you go to bed?
4. If you ..... leave your bags and cameras here, please, ladies and gentlemen.
5. Look, stop shouting at me, ..... you?!

LET'S *(AZ 219)*

***6. Faites des suggestions en utilisant*** let's ***à la forme affirmative ou négative selon le cas.***

1. I feel really thirsty. *(have a drink)*
2. I don't like this bar. *(try somewhere else)*
3. I hate buses. *(not catch a bus ; take a taxi)*
4. I'm tired. *(go home)*
5. No, *(not go home yet ; have some fun)*

EXCLAMATIONS : **HOW ...! ET WHAT ...!** *(AZ 132)*

***7. Remettez dans le bon ordre les éléments des phrases suivantes en ajoutant*** how ***ou*** what ***selon le cas.***

1. eyes / ..... / beautiful !
2. awful / ..... !
3. life / ..... / sad / a !
4. ..... / luck / terrible !
5. have / sister / ..... / a / you / nice !
6. this / ..... / is / annoying !
7. was / She / realise / ..... / a / man / didn't / he / kind .
8. is / you / Have / ..... / noticed / quiet / it ?

EXCLAMATIONS : **ISN'T ...!, AREN'T ...!** *(AZ 133)*

***8. Transformez les phrases suivantes en exclamations à l'aide de*** Isn't ...! ***etc.***

1. That's a fantastic car.
2. She's got beautiful hair.
3. Those cakes look delicious.
4. You've been wonderful.
5. He was charming.
6. It will be exciting.
7. This town has changed.
8. You're proud of your children.
9. They showed great courage.
10. She sings well.

6. 'Is Tony not with you?' 'No, he ..*(not)*.. come. He said he was tired.'
7. 'Give us the papers!' 'No, we ..*(not)*..!'
8. Ladies and gentlemen, ..... you please welcome – Johnny Dalleyhay!!!!

FUTUR ANTÉRIEUR *(AZ 153)*

***6. Pat et Sean sont sur le point de partir pour un grand voyage touristique. Lisez attentivement leur plan de voyage, puis écrivez des phrases en utilisant le futur antérieur simple ou progressif.***

**Ex. :** By the end of January / they / visit *(country?)*
*By the end of January they will have visited France.*

**January:** France **February:** Spain and Portugal
**March:** Morocco **April:** Egypt **May:** Israel
**June:** Turkey and Greece **July:** Italy
**August:** Switzerland and Germany
**September:** home (Ireland)

1. After three months / they / see *(number?)* countries
2. By the beginning of *(month?)* / they / go to the pyramids
3. By the end of July / they / travel for *(number?)* months
4. In eight months' time / they / visit *(number?)* countries
5. By the middle of September / they / return home to *(country?)*

FUTUR PROGRESSIF *(AZ 154)*

***7. Regardez attentivement l'agenda de Brigitte à la page de demain matin. Utilisez le futur progressif pour dire ce qu'elle sera en train de faire aux heures indiquées.***

**Ex. :** 7.25 *She'll be travelling by train to London.*

**Tuesday 24 May**

*7.20 Train to London*
*8.30 See Joe Richards*
*9.45 Interview new secretary*
*11.00 Discuss new brochure with Peter*
*11.15 Phone John Brown*
*11.30 Read business reports*
*12.45 Lunch with Sarah Johnson*

1. 8.35
2. 9.50
3. 11.05
4. 11.20
5. 11.35
6. 12.50

BE + TO-INFINITIF *(AZ 60)*

***8. Complétez les phrases en utilisant*** be to ***à la forme qui convient.***

1. The President ..... address the Senate at 3.30 today.
2. I left the office early because I ..... meet the children after school.
3. He didn't know it at the time, but she was the woman he ..... marry.
4. They ..... travel by train but all services were stopped because of the bad weather.
5. Daddy says you ..... go upstairs and get dressed for bed – immediately!
6. This medicine ..... be taken after meals.
7. According to this we ..... leave at 9.30 and arrive two hours later. We'd better hurry!
8. Remember you ..*(not)*.. do any work at all – just take it really easy!

ABOUT TO *(AZ 3)*

***9. Complétez les dialogues à l'aide de*** just be about to ***(présent ou prétérit). Utilisez des contractions lorsque c'est possible.***

1. 'Hasn't she left yet?' 'She ..... leave now.'
2. 'Would you open the window, please?' 'I ..... open it.'
3. 'Haven't the children gone to bed yet?' 'They ..... go to bed now.'
4. 'Can Tony come out to play?' 'Sorry, he ..... have his dinner.'
5. 'Have you written to Mrs Evans?' 'I ..... write to her now.'
6. 'I'm really sorry I'm late!' 'We ..... go home.'
7. 'Has Paul phoned Tom yet?' 'He ..... phone him now.'

FUTUR DANS LE PASSÉ *(AZ 155)*

***10. Récrivez ces phrases en commençant par les mots en italique. Utilisez le futur dans le passé.***

1. They'll win their match. *I didn't think ...*
2. He's going to give up smoking. *His mother was delighted to hear ...*

3. The plane doesn't take off until 12.30. *There wasn't any hurry because ...*
4. She's doing an exam in the morning. *She went to bed early because ...*
5. We are to stay here. *Who told you ...?*
6. They are going to move to Australia. *The last time I talked to them ...*
7. My music lesson finishes at 6.15. *There wasn't going to be much time because ...*
8. The Prime Minister is to visit Liverpool in April. *It said on TV ...*
9. He'll be all right. *We all hoped ...*
10. They're coming on Saturday. *How did you know ...?*

EXERCICE DE SYNTHÈSE *(AZ 148-152, 352, 410)*

***11. Complétez les phrases suivantes à l'aide de*** will***,*** shall***,*** be going to***, le présent simple ou le présent progressif. Il y a parfois plusieurs possibilités. Utilisez des contractions lorsque c'est possible.***

1. 'Look at those clouds! It *(snow)*, I reckon.' 'Mmm. I think I *(get)* my coat. *(I, get)* yours too?' 'Thanks. We *(need)* them!'

2. 'Are you free tomorrow at 10?' 'Well, my violin lesson *(start)* at 10.15, and then I *(meet)* Joe at about 11.30 ... Look. I *(ring)* you next week and we *(organise)* something then. OK?' 'Or *(I, phone)* you?' 'Yeah, OK. I *(be)* at home every evening this week.' 'Right. I *(talk)* to you on Tuesday then.' 'Fine. I've got to go now. My brother *(come)* round in a minute.' 'Bye.'

3. 'If you tell her, I *(never speak)* to you again.' 'Stop panicking, ..... you? I *(not tell)* anybody. But in return, *(you, help)* me?' 'What do you want?' 'Tell me where the money is.' 'No, I ..... Never!'

4. 'What *(we, do)* today?' 'Let's go into town.' '*(we, take)* the car?' 'I'm afraid it *(not start)*.' 'OK, then. I *(call)* a taxi. *(I, ask)* for it for 11 o'clock?' 'No. *(you, tell)* them to come a bit later than that? I'm not ready yet.' 'Right. I *(phone)* the taxi company now.'

→

5. 'What time *(the bus, go)*?' 'Not until 2.15.' 'Great! I *(have)* a cup of tea.' '*(you, get)* me one too, please?' '*(I, buy)* you something to eat as well?' 'Yeah, OK.' 'Right, I *(not be)* long.'

EXERCICE DE SYNTHÈSE *(AZ 153-155, 60, 3)*

**12. Complétez les phrases à l'aide des expressions ci-dessous.**

| |
|---|
| 'll be flying are about to are to is to was about to wasn't going were going Will you be needing Will you have decided will have finished will have used wouldn't forget |

1. Come and visit us in April. We ..... redecorating by then.
2. ..... the computer after lunch or can I use it?
3. The children ..... go to bed at 9.00 – no later.
4. This time next week we ..... to Egypt on holiday. I can't wait!
5. I ..... say hello to her when I realised it wasn't her at all.
6. I knew he ..... to like it.
7. The Pope ..... visit China next year.
8. We hoped she ....., but unfortunately she did.
9. By 2050 there won't be any oil left in the world: we ..... it all up.
10. Come quickly: they ..... leave.
11. The first time we met, they ..... to move to New Zealand.
12. ..... what to do by the end of the month?

# 20 Le passif

PASSIF : FORMATION *(AZ 281)*

***1. Donnez la forme passive des verbes suivants.***

1. to use
2. I am teaching
3. you choose
4. he killed
5. she was calling
6. we have taken
7. they had eaten
8. I will meet
9. it would break
10. you will have brought
11. she would have forgotten
12. hearing

PASSIF : EMPLOI *(AZ 282)*

***2. Construisez des phrases au passif à l'aide des éléments fournis. Attention aux temps.***

1. Radioactivity / discover / Marie and Pierre Curie / at the end of the 19th century
2. Spanish / speak in Brazil?
3. The money / already spend (present perfect)
4. Workers / soon replace / robots
5. How many people / kill / on the roads every year?
6. When / you / interview / tomorrow?
7. The Eiffel Tower / build / 1889 / Gustave Eiffel
8. Cheese / make / from milk
9. He / not see / since 1985
10. Your car / repair / at the moment

**GET** + PARTICIPE PASSÉ *(AZ 158)*

***3. Transformez les phrases suivantes en utilisant*** get ***+ participe passé.***

1. My dinner was eaten by the cat.
2. It'll be stolen if you are not careful!
3. We are always asked to the Christmas party.

→

4. Have you ever been arrested?
5. All the windows had been broken.

PASSIF : VERBES À DEUX COMPLÉMENTS OU SUIVIS D'UNE PROPOSITION INFINITIVE *(AZ 283, 284)*

***4. Traduisez en anglais.***

1. On m'a donné un prix *(= prize)* magnifique. (prétérit)
2. On vous prêtera £1,000.
3. On a acheté une nouvelle voiture à Nicole. (present perfect)
4. On leur avait promis de l'avancement. *(= promotion)*
5. On nous apprend l'allemand le mardi soir.
6. On vous a interdit de partir. (present perfect)
7. On me demande très souvent de lire mes poèmes.
8. On avait dit à John de rester à la maison.
9. On te demandera de jouer de la guitare.
10. On les a fait venir très tôt. (prétérit)

EXERCICE DE SYNTHÈSE *(AZ 281-284, 158)*

***5. Mettez les verbes entre parenthèses au passif, au temps qui convient. Utilisez*** get ***au lieu de*** be ***lorsque c'est indiqué.***

1. **The exam**
   'When I arrived, I *(ask)* to wait outside the interview room with the other students. I wanted a cigarette but we *(not allow)* to smoke.' '*(you, make)* to wait for a long time?' 'About ten minutes, but then I *(invite)* to go in.' 'What *(you, get, ask)* to do?' 'Well, I *(show)* some pictures and I *(expect)* to talk about them.' 'In Italian?' 'Yeah, and the whole thing *(record)*.' 'When *(the results, announce)*?' 'They *(announce)* already – I passed!'
2. **A day in France**
   'Hey look! We *(send)* the details of the day trip to France. We *(get, pick up)* at the bus station at six o'clock on Friday morning and then we *(drive)* to Dover. We *(get, meet)* on the ship by the guide and we *(serve)* breakfast in the restaurant. At Boulogne we *(get, take)* on a tour around the city and we *(invite)* to a concert after lunch.' 'Great! But *(we, expect)* to speak French all the time?!'

3. **Another burglary *(= cambriolage )*!**
'I'm terribly sorry – I hear you *(get, burgle)* last night.' 'Yes, I'm afraid so. When we got home from work, we found that the bathroom window *(break)*. The alarm *(disconnect)* – I don't know how!' 'What *(steal)*?' 'Well, nothing *(get, take)*, but a lot of things *(damage)*. Our house is the third house in the road which *(burgle)* this month.' '*(anyone, catch)* yet?' 'I don't know. We *(not tell)* anything.'

## 21 La phrase : structures de base

QUESTIONS : RÈGLES DE BASE *(AZ 339)*

***1. Vous venez de faire connaissance avec un Anglais / une Anglaise à Paris. Reformulez correctement vos questions.***

1. 'When / you / get here?' 'Yesterday.'
2. 'How / you / travel?' 'By plane.'
3. 'You / been to Paris before?' 'Yes, last year.'
4. 'You / speak French ?' 'Yes, quite well.'
5. 'Where / you / staying?' 'With some friends of mine.'
6. 'Where / they / live?' 'Near Montmartre.'
7. 'You / been up the Eiffel Tower?' 'No, not yet.'
8. 'You / like French food?' 'Yes, I love it.'
9. 'What / you / going to do next?' 'Visit the Louvre.'
10. 'How long / you / staying in Paris?' 'A week.'
11. 'What / you / do?' 'I'm a doctor.'
12. 'You / like / to have coffee with me?' 'I'd love to!'

QUESTIONS : INTERRONÉGATION *(AZ 341)*

**2. *Complétez les dialogues en utilisant les formes interronégatives ci-dessous.***

**Ex. :** 'She's very lonely.' *'Hasn't she got any friends?'*

| | | | | | | |
|---|---|---|---|---|---|---|
| Aren't | Didn't | didn't | didn't | doesn't | Don't | Hasn't |
| Hasn't | Haven't | Isn't | | | | |

1. 'They're not coming to the party.' 'Why ..... they tell us?'
2. 'I don't know where he is.' '..... you received news from him yet?'
3. 'He makes the same mistake every time.' 'Why ..... he look at the instructions?'
4. 'It's difficult being so far away from her.' '..... you going to visit her next February?'
5. 'I didn't buy that dress.' '..... you like it?'
6. 'There isn't any paper left.' '..... there more in the desk?'
7. 'Not everyone was there.' 'Who ..... come?'
8. 'I'm sorry, I hate this kind of music.' '..... you like jazz?'
9. 'Let's buy this book for Ann.' '..... she read it already?'

**HOW LONG / TALL,** ETC. ...? *(AZ 182, 184, 185)*

**3. *Posez les questions commençant par* How *qui correspondent aux réponses suivantes.***

1. We're staying here until next May.
2. Mont Blanc? Nearly 5,000 metres.
3. He'd been ill for a long time.
4. The Great Wall of China? Just over 4,000 kilometres.
5. They've been playing computer games since lunchtime.
6. The Suez Canal? At least 60 metres.
7. We see each other every six months.
8. The Sun from the Earth? About 150 million kilometres.
9. I've been skiing three or four times.
10. The nearest garage? Less than half a mile.
11. She's only five feet.
12. It's not very cold.

NÉGATION *(AZ 249)*

***4. Rendez les phrases suivantes négatives à l'aide des mots entre parenthèses. Utilisez des contractions si la phrase le permet.***

1. She eats chocolate. *(not)*
2. I like her. *(not)*
3. He's at home. *(never)*
4. I go to the seaside during the winter. *(never)*
5. We see Tom at weekends. *(not)*
6. They know everything. *(not)*
7. He says hello to everybody. *(not)*
8. We drink tea and coffee. *(neither … nor)*
9. She can stand up. *(hardly)*
10. You visit your mother. *(hardly ever)*
11. I spend some time with him. *(hardly)*
12. They finished the exercises with some difficulty. *(without)*

IMPÉRATIF *(AZ 190)*

***5. Vous donnez des conseils en matière de santé. Complétez les phrases suivantes en utilisant les verbes ci-dessous à l'impératif affirmatif ou négatif.***

| |
|---|
| brush drink eat (x 2) forget get go out live remember start stay stop |

1. ..... smoking.
2. ..... lots of fresh vegetables.
3. ..*(never)*.. too much tea or coffee.
4. ..*(always)*.. your teeth *(= dents)* after every meal.
5. ..... to drink lots of water every day.
6. ..... to do some exercise every week.
7. ..*(always)*.. enough sleep.
8. ..... too many cakes or too much meat.
9. ..*(never)*.. in the hot sun without wearing a hat and some suncream.
10. ..... healthy – ..... longer!

QUESTIONS ET EXCLAMATIONS *(AZ 339, 132)*

**9. *Transformez les questions en exclamations, et les exclamations en questions.***

1. How difficult this is!
2. How hard are they working?
3. How lucky you've been!
4. How interesting was it?
5. How easy it's going to be!
6. How well did they play?
7. How quickly you do it!
8. How busy is she?
9. How beautiful it will look!
10. How nice has the weather been?

**THERE IS** *(AZ 383)*

**10. *Complétez les phrases à l'aide des formes ci-dessous.***

| | | |
|---|---|---|
| there is/ are | there was/ were | there has/ have been |
| there will be | there's going to be | there must be |
| there might be | there would be | there used to be |

1. ..... enough food for everyone in the world but unfortunately ..... also too many greedy people in the world.
2. According to these plans ..... a new shopping centre where my old school used to be.
3. ..... twenty coal mines in this region, but now there are only two.
4. ..... a phone call for you earlier this morning and ..... two more this afternoon.
5. I don't think ..... another world war in the next twenty years, but .....
6. Here is the 1 o'clock news. ..... a big explosion in New York and ..... more fires in Los Angeles ...
7. ..... a way to stop all this killing.
8. I told him that if he tried to do anything to stop me, ..... a lot of trouble.

THERE IS *(AZ 383)*

***11. Transformez ces phrases affirmatives en phrases négatives (N) ou en questions (Q). Utilisez des contractions lorsque c'est possible.***

**Ex. :** There is a god. (**Q**) *Is there a god?*

1. There were a lot of people. (**N**)
2. There might be a problem with this. (**Q**)
3. There will be snow in the mountains. (**N**)
4. There has been a revolution in Pakistan. (**Q**)
5. There should be more help for the poor. (**N**)
6. There would be an ecological disaster if this nuclear power station exploded. (**Q**)
7. There used to be a cinema in this town. (**N**)
8. There are going to be too many people at the party. (**Q**)
9. There are a lot of cars on the island. (**N**)
10. There was a good film on TV last night. (**Q**)
11. There have been many complaints *(= plaintes)* against the hospital. (**N**)

## 22 Tags : question-tags, reprises interrogatives, réponses courtes

QUESTION-TAGS *(AZ 375)*

***1. Vous êtes agent de police. Vous voulez confirmer quelques renseignements sur un suspect. Questionnez-le en utilisant les tags ci-dessous.***

**Ex. :** Your name / be / Simon Jones

*Your name is Simon Jones, isn't it?*

| | | | | |
|---|---|---|---|---|
| are you | aren't you (x 2) | can't you | did he | do you |
| hasn't she | have you (x 2) | haven't you | isn't it | |
| wasn't he | wasn't it | weren't you (x 2) | | |

1. You / be / 31 years old
2. You / not come from London
3. You / not be / married
4. You / live with your girlfriend since January (present perfect progressif)
5. She / be away for the last few weeks (present perfect)
6. You / not have a job at the moment
7. You / be in the army five years ago (prétérit)
8. You / can use a gun
9. You / never be in prison (present perfect)
10. You / be in The Red Lion pub last night (prétérit)
11. It / be after 10.30 (prétérit)
12. Tony Smith / be with you (prétérit)
13. He / not give you anything (prétérit)
14. You / stay in town for the next few weeks

QUESTION-TAGS *(AZ 375)*

***2. Poursuivez l'interrogatoire avec un autre suspect, Tony Smith. Complétez ces phrases à l'aide de question-tags.***

1. Sit down, .....
2. Let's have a little talk, .....
3. You know why you're here, .....
4. You met Jones at The Red Lion, .....
5. He gave you a small box, .....
6. It contained drugs, .....

→

7. You paid him £10,000, .....
8. He had a gun, .....
9. He wanted more money, .....
10. You know where his girlfriend is, .....
11. I'm right, .....
12. Answer me, .....

REPRISES INTERROGATIVES *(AZ 376)*

***3. Ces phrases ont été coupées en deux. Reconstituez-les.***

**Ex. :** *1 – c*

| | |
|---|---|
| 1. 'Your letter hasn't arrived yet.' | a. 'Wasn't it?' |
| 2. 'You just aren't good enough.' | b. 'Must you?' |
| 3. 'They've already had breakfast.' | c. 'Hasn't it?' |
| 4. 'It wasn't ready on time.' | d. 'Do we?' |
| 5. 'You're going to do as you are told.' | e. 'Aren't I?' |
| 6. 'We weren't very happy.' | f. 'Have they?' |
| 7. 'We really must go.' | g. 'Can't she?' |
| 8. 'You both look wonderful!' | h. 'Am I?' |
| 9. 'She can't swim.' | i. 'Weren't you?' |

RÉPONSES COURTES *(AZ 377)*

***4. Ces phrases ont été coupées en deux. Reconstituez-les.***

**A**

| | |
|---|---|
| 1. 'He doesn't like you.' | a. 'No, she won't.' |
| 2. 'Will she be sorry to leave?' | b. 'We will.' |
| 3. 'This is completely wrong.' | c. 'No, they weren't.' |
| 4. 'Weren't they happy with it?' | d. 'No, it isn't.' |
| 5. 'We won't have enough money.' | e. 'You're right, he doesn't.' |

**B**

| | |
|---|---|
| 1. 'Can't you help her?' | a. 'I didn't.' |
| 2. 'She loved travelling.' | b. 'They had.' |
| 3. 'I'm going to the concert.' | c. 'Yes, I did.' |
| 4. 'I'd go by plane if I had the choice.' | d. 'Yes, we can.' |
| 5. 'You didn't remember her birthday.' | e. 'I would have.' |
| 6. 'We wouldn't have told them.' | f. 'We aren't.' |
| 7. 'He hadn't eaten there before.' | g. 'I wouldn't.' |

RÉPONSES COURTES AVEC **SO** ET **NEITHER/NOR** ; MOI AUSSI ...
*(AZ 378, 57)*

***5. C'est le premier rendez-vous de Michel avec son chef de service, Sophie. Il donne raison à tout ce qu'elle lui dit. Écrivez toutes les possibilités.***

**Ex. :** 'I like this restaurant.' *'Me too.' / 'I do too.' / 'So do I.'*

1. 'But I can't stand the decor.'
2. 'I'm a vegetarian.'
3. 'But I still eat fish.'
4. 'I've never eaten crab.'
5. 'And I'm not going to try it this time either.'
6. 'I wouldn't choose the spaghetti.'
7. 'I think I'll have the fish.'
8. 'But I'm having some soup first.'
9. 'I've always hated red wine.'
10. 'I won't order *(= commander)* dessert until later.'
11. 'I really respect people who have their own opinions.'

## 23 Discours indirect

DISCOURS INDIRECT *(AZ 103)*

***1. Une nouvelle Présidente vient d'être élue. Rapportez ses déclarations.***

**Ex. :** 'It's the happiest day of my life.' *She said ...*
*She said it was the happiest day of her life.'*

1. 'I have dreamed about becoming President for a very long time.' *She told us she ...*
2. 'It's the start of a new age.' *Every new President says ...*
3. 'There will be great changes.' *She promised that ...*
4. 'We won't need to increase taxes.'
   *She doesn't think they ...*
5. 'We're going to conquer inflation.'
   *All politicians say they ...*
6. 'We're going to bring down unemployment.'
   *She said they ...*
7. 'I've always been against nuclear weapons.'
   *She told us she ...*
8. 'I want to bring peace to the world.' *She said she ...* →

9. 'I will do my best for the country.' *She promised that she ...*
10. 'Work with me for a better future!' *She asked us ...*
11. 'Never lose hope!' *She told us ...*

DISCOURS INDIRECT (MODAUX) *(AZ 103)*

***2. Retrouvez les termes exacts du discours prononcé par la nouvelle Présidente.***

**Ex. :** She told us that we could all enjoy a better life.
*'We/ You can all enjoy a better life.'*

1. She said we must all work together.
2. She told us that it might be difficult at times.
3. She said that we should be strong.
4. She said that we shouldn't give up hope.
5. She said we ought to give her our support *(= soutien).*
6. She told us we could count on her.

DISCOURS INDIRECT : LES INTERROGATIONS *(AZ 104)*

***3. Vous venez d'avoir une entrevue avec la nouvelle Présidente. Rapportez les questions que vous lui avez posées en commençant toujours par*** I asked her.

1. 'Is this really the happiest day of your life?'
2. 'What sort of changes are you planning?'
3. 'Will you reduce taxation?'
4. 'Can you really conquer inflation?'
5. 'What are you going to do about unemployment?'
6. 'How long have you been against nuclear weapons?'
7. 'Will you really bring peace to the world?'
8. 'How will the future be better?'
9. 'Do you see difficult times in the years to come?'
10. 'How hopeful are you?'

DISCOURS INDIRECT : PRONOMS, DÉTERMINANTS ET ADVERBES *(AZ 105, 103)*

***4. Mettez les phrases suivantes au discours indirect, en faisant très attention aux changements de pronoms, déterminants et adverbes.***

1. 'You're an idiot, Tom!' *I told Tom ...*
2. 'Do you want these books?' *He asked me if ...*

3. 'What are you doing tomorrow?' *We asked them what …*
4. 'He wasn't at work last week.' *His wife told me …*
5. 'Does he still live here?' *She asked them if …*
6. 'Where were you yesterday?' *I asked her where …*
7. 'We phoned you two days ago.' *They told him …*
8. 'Is he going to Paris next week?' *They asked her if …*

**SAY** ET **TELL** *(AZ 349)*

***5. Remplacez*** say ***par*** tell ***et*** tell ***par*** say ***chaque fois que c'est possible. Faites les autres modifications nécessaires.***

**Ex. :** She said two things to me. *She told me two things.*

1. They told me nothing.
2. 'Leave us alone,' they said to him.
3. Come on: tell me the truth!
4. What did they say to you?
5. Please, tell me a story.
6. He's always telling lies.
7. Say it to him before he goes.
8. They told us there was a problem.
9. She loves telling jokes.

EXERCICE DE SYNTHÈSE *(AZ 103-105, 349)*

***6. Mettez les phrases du dialogue entre Anne et Paul au discours indirect en faisant toutes les modifications nécessaires.***

1. 'I can't come to the concert on Tuesday,' she said.
2. 'Why didn't you tell me before?' he asked.
3. 'I've been very busy,' she said.
4. 'I bought the tickets *(= billets)* two weeks ago,' he said.
5. 'Tony might like to go,' she said.
6. 'I'd prefer to go with you,' he said.
7. 'I've got to travel to Paris on business,' she said.
8. 'When are you leaving?' he asked.
9. 'I'm flying on Tuesday morning,' she said.
10. 'Are you staying for long?' he asked.
11. 'I should be back next week,' she said.
12. 'Will you send me a postcard?' he asked.
13. 'Will you phone me in Paris?' she asked.
14. 'Bring me back a bottle of cognac,' he said.

IF + PRÉSENT OU PRÉTÉRIT *(AZ 186)*

***1. Les phrases suivantes ont été coupées en deux. Reconstituez-les. Il y a parfois plusieurs combinaisons possibles.***

| | |
|---|---|
| 1. If I don't spend more time at home, | a. I'd probably eat out more. |
| 2. If we get a new government, | b. I'd possibly become ill. |
| 3. If I became President, | c. everyone will be very surprised. |
| 4. If I didn't have ears, | d. I won't have to go to work tomorrow. |
| 5. If I become fatter, | e. I'd possibly be more popular with women. |
| 6. If I worked harder, | f. a lot of things will change in this country. |
| 7. If the world ends tonight, | g. I probably wouldn't be any happier. |
| 8. If I don't finish this work today, | h. it would be a big mistake. |
| 9. If I had more money, | i. my husband will probably leave me. |
| 10. If lived in Paris, | j. I'll have to change all my clothes. |
| 11. If the weather is good this summer, | k. my glasses would fall off. |
| 12. If I was tall, dark and good-looking, | l. I'll be in big trouble. |

***Choisissez six des propositions subordonnées (colonne de gauche) et complétez-les de manière à exprimer votre point de vue.***

**IF** + PLUPERFECT *(AZ 186)*

***2. Joe a dû modifier ses projets de vacances. Utilisez*** if ***+ pluperfect pour évoquer ce qui avait été prévu.***

**Ex. :** He wanted to go to France, but he didn't have enough money.

*He would have gone to France if he had had enough money.*

1. He had intended to go with his girlfriend, but they broke up just before the holiday.
2. He hadn't wanted to go with his brother, Paul, but there was no one else free at the time.
3. They had planned to cycle everywhere, but Tom hurt his leg.
4. They had hoped to camp a lot, but the weather was awful.
5. They had expected to visit lots of interesting places, but Paul fell ill.
6. They had intended to stay for two weeks but they spent all their money after ten days.

**IF** : CAS PARTICULIERS *(AZ 187)*

***3. Traduisez en anglais.***

1. Si vous voulez avoir l'obligeance d'informer *(= inform)* votre femme que nous l'attendons en bas …
2. Je me suis demandé s'ils arriveraient à l'heure *(= on time)*.
3. Nous ne savons pas si nous serons libres demain.
4. Veux-tu venir avec moi? Si oui, dépêche-toi!
5. On a assez de vin? Sinon j'en acheterai encore quelques bouteilles.
6. Nous resterons ici s'il le faut.
7. À votre place je ne leur dirais pas un mot.
8. Si par hasard vous vous perdiez *(= get lost)*, n'hésitez pas à nous téléphoner.

**UNLESS ; WHETHER** *(AZ 392, 406)*

***4. Transformez ces phrases à l'aide de*** unless ***ou*** whether.

1. We'll stay here if the weather doesn't improve.
2. If we don't hurry, we'll miss the plane.
3. I never go out in the sun if I'm not wearing a hat.

→

4. Do you remember if you gave them the address?
5. If you don't make an effort, there'll be trouble!
6. Young people these days – you can't tell if they're boys or girls!
7. He never contacts me if there isn't a problem.
8. They'll come by train if they can't get a bus.
9. Ask them if they want to come with us or go with Joe.

EXERCICE DE SYNTHÈSE *(AZ 186, 187, 392, 406)*

***5. Choisissez la forme qui convient. Parfois les deux sont possibles.***

1. 'If he *comes/ will come*, he*'ll/ 'd* have a great time.' 'He's not sure *if/whether* he'll have time. *If so/ If not*, he'll probably come next time.' '*If/ Unless* he's busy then too!' 'Well, *if/ whether* he comes or not, we're going to enjoy ourselves!'
2. 'If you *don't/ didn't* have to work, how would you spend your day?' 'I think I*'ll/ 'd* stay in bed.' 'And if there *was/ would be* a good football match on ...?' 'Ah, that *will/ would* be different!'
3. If I *knew/ had known* then what I know now, I *would never get/ would never have got* married!
4. 'If you *would/ should* see him, give him my love.' 'If I *was/were* you, I *will/ would* try to forget him.'
5. *If/ Unless* countries don't cooperate more, there *will/ would* never be peace in the world.

**WHEN** + PRÉSENT OU FUTUR *(AZ 405)*

***1. Choisissez la forme verbale qui convient.***

1. 'When *do/ will* you get a company car?' 'When they *make/ will make* me a manager. I'm not sure when that *is/ will be*. Perhaps when we *move/ will move* to the new offices.'
2. 'What will you do when the money *is/ will be* all gone?' 'I'll worry about that when the time *comes/ will come.*' 'When *do/ will* you ever learn?' 'When *do/ will* you ever learn to leave me alone?!'
3. 'I think I'll go straight to bed when I *get/ will get* home.' 'When *do/ will* you ring me?' 'Tomorrow, when I *get/ will get* into the office.'

TEMPS APRÈS **WHEN, AFTER, ...** *(AZ 156)*

***2. Choisissez la forme verbale qui convient.***

1. When the weather *gets / will get* better, we'll go swimming.
2. Don't say a word to anybody who *will talk / talks* you.
3. I'll let you know as soon as she *calls / will call.*
4. The tourist guides will take you wherever you *will want / want* to go to.
5. We'll be satisfied as long as you *have done / will have done* your best.
6. I'll give you more when you *will have eaten / have eaten* what you have now.
7. They'll let us know as soon as they *will have completed/ have completed* all the tests.
8. My parents told me they would like to travel more after they *would stop / stopped* working.
9. If I were him I would take the money before his boss *changed / would change* her mind.
10. She would have helped me if I *would have asked / had asked* her to.
11. You promised to meet us in the hotel foyer after you *had had / would have had* a shower.
12. They said they wouldn't stop until they *would have finished / had finished* the job.

SINCE *(AZ 358, 100)*

***3. Reliez les phrases à l'aide de* since *et des mots proposés.***

**Ex. :** We got married in 1985. We are still married. *(be married) We've been married since 1985.*

1. It started raining on Thursday. It's still raining. *(rain)*
2. She moved to Australia as a child. She's still there. *(live)*
3. He met her just before he started university. He's still at university. He hasn't seen her again. *(not see)*
4. We played football at school. We've left school now. *(not play)*
5. I last visited my aunt when I was ten. She died last week. *(not visit)*

SINCE : IT IS/ WAS ... SINCE *(AZ 359, 100)*

***4. Transformez les phrases suivantes à l'aide de* It's/ It was ... since.**

**Ex. :** We haven't been to the theatre for ages.
*It's ages since we went to the theatre.*

1. I had a letter from him five weeks ago.
2. You haven't looked so well for a long time.
3. They last talked to each other more than a month ago.
4. I hadn't worked with him for over fifteen years.
5. The children hadn't had a proper meal for days.

***Complétez la phrase suivante de manière à exprimer votre pensée.***
It's ages since ...

CONJONCTIONS *(AZ 27, 46-48, 192, 364, 407)*

***5. Complétez les phrases suivantes en utilisant les expressions ci-dessous.***

| | | | | |
|---|---|---|---|---|
| as | as if | as long as | even though | in case |
| provided that | so that | until | whereas | while |

1. We kept very quiet ..... my parents shouldn't hear us.
2. Can you listen to music ..... you are working?
3. Don't do anything ..... he tells you to.

4. They closed all the doors and windows ..... anyone should try to get in.
5. She can't speak French ..... she's lived in Paris for years.
6. We decided not to invite them ..... they had never invited us.
7. She worries a lot ..... I'm quite relaxed.
8. It looks ..... we haven't got any petrol left.
9. There'll be no trouble ..... they follow our instructions.
10. We'll keep you here ..... we want to.

CONJONCTIONS *(AZ 27, 46-48, 192, 364, 407)*

***6. Complétez les phrases à l'aide des mots et expressions ci-dessous en mettant les verbes entre parenthèses aux temps qui conviennent. Il y a parfois plusieurs possibilités.***

| | | | | | |
|---|---|---|---|---|---|
| although | as long as | as though | in case | in order that | |
| in spite of | since | so long as | though | until | while |

1. She won't stop ..... the job *(be)* finished.
2. ..... he was very enthusiastic about the idea, I thought it was completely crazy.
3. We'll wait for you ..... we *(can)*.
4. All right. I'll tell you ..... you seem to want to know.
5. ..... she's in her seventies she's still got lots of energy.
6. I carried the vase very carefully ..... it *(not get)* broken.
7. We'll let you stay ..... you *(not make)* any noise.
8. I feel ..... this could be the end of our relationship.
9. I'll phone Bob ..... he *(feel)* like joining us.
10. The food wasn't very good. The wine was nice, ......
11. He's still very optimistic ..... everything.

# 26 L'ordre des mots

PLACE DES ADVERBES : À CÔTÉ DU VERBE *(AZ 290)*

***1. Corrigez les phrases en remettant l'adverbe à sa place la plus courante.***

1. We spend usually our holidays in Brittany.
2. He is talking probably to her now.
3. We also were very pleased.
4. I have heard just your news.
5. You visit us rarely these days.
6. Take drugs never.
7. They are doctors both.
8. She rang me hardly ever.
9. We are going certainly to complain.
10. They have finished nearly their work.
11. It mainly was a financial question.
12. If he had married her he would have been still unhappy.

PLACE DES ADVERBES : À CÔTÉ DU VERBE *(AZ 290)*

***2. Mettez les mots dans le bon ordre.***

1. see / did / last / When / them / you ?
2. don't / know / I / him / certainly .
3. that / Do / hat / always / wear / you ?
4. hello / She / say / even / didn't .
5. really / Has / it / he / lost ?
6. coming / probably / They / aren't .
7. English / speak / Can / only / she ?
8. London / Are / still / to / you / live / in / going ?

PLACE DES ADVERBES : **PERHAPS** ET **MAYBE ; VERY MUCH, ... ;** COMPLÉMENTS EN FIN DE PHRASE *(AZ 291-293)*

***3. Mettez les mots entre parenthèses à la place qui convient.***

1. We don't swim in the winter. *(very much)*
2. I don't eat meat. *(at all)*
3. We were talking too much. *(perhaps)*
4. He always used to play tennis. *(very well)*
5. They travel to the USA. *(a lot)*

6. She couldn't get a babysitter. *(maybe)*
7. I prefer eating at home to going out to eat. *(very much)*
8. He was at a meeting yesterday. *(in Bordeaux)*
9. I'll ring you at home. *(later)*
10. Did you sleep last night? *(well)*
11. We worked together very successfully in 1987. *(at the Oxford branch)*
12. They fell very much in love in Greece. *(last summer)*

**ENOUGH ; HALF ; QUITE ; RATHER ; SO** ET **SUCH**
*(AZ 126, 165, 342, 343, 362)*

**4. Mettez les mots entre parenthèses à la place qui convient.**

1. Do you think we've got wine for the party? *(enough)*
2. There's a bottle of milk in the fridge. *(half)*
3. She's a good teacher. *(quite)*
4. I like walking to work. *(rather)*
5. It's a difficult decision. *(rather)*
6. We had a good time. *(such)*

VERBE + PARTICULE *(AZ 398)*

**5. Récrivez les phrases soulignées en modifiant l'ordre des mots quand c'est possible.**

**Ex. :** Please turn the light off. Please turn off the light.

1. Try not to wake up the dog!
2. I liked your moustache. Why did you cut it off?
3. 'Where's Tom's letter?' 'I've thrown it away.'
4. We looked the words up in the dictionary.
5. The children are trying to sleep. Could you turn down the TV a bit, please?
6. I hadn't talked to her for a long time, so I decided to ring her up.
7. She wrote her address down and gave it to him.
8. It's a lovely dress. Why don't you try it on?

VERBES À DEUX COMPLÉMENTS *(AZ 396)*

***6. Récrivez les phrases comme dans les exemples. (Certaines phrases ne peuvent pas être modifiées.)***

**Ex. :** Could you buy me a newspaper, please?
*Could you buy a newspaper for me, please?*
**Ex. :** I wrote a long letter to John. *I wrote John a long letter.*

1. She's been teaching German to my children for over a year.
2. Please, would you tell Sarah a story?
3. Can you describe the car to me?
4. She offered a job to my father.
5. I'd like to suggest a different plan to you.
6. They showed us their house.
7. Did you give the keys to them?
8. Would you explain this word to me?
9. I'll send you the details tomorrow.
10. Open the window for me, will you?

INVERSION : ANGLAIS FORMEL *(AZ 207)*

***7. Récrivez les phrases de façon plus formelle en commençant par les mots entre parenthèses.***

1. If anything goes wrong, please ring this number. *(Should anything …)*
2. I got into the bath. The phone immediately rang. *(No sooner …)*
3. (He shut the door.) That was when he realised he'd left the keys inside. *(Only then …)*
4. I've never in my life regretted becoming an engineer. *(At no time …)*
5. If I was in his position, I wouldn't stay in that job any longer. *(Were I …)*
6. They arrived late, and they didn't even say sorry! *(Not only …)*
7. Her mother died. That was when she found out the terrible truth. *(Only after her mother's death …)*
8. We left the house. It immediately started raining. *(Hardly …)*
9. If they'd told me there was a problem, I'd certainly have helped them. *(Had they …)*

INVERSION : EN FRANÇAIS, PAS EN ANGLAIS *(AZ 208)*

**8. *Les éléments des phrases suivantes ont été mélangés. Remettez-les dans le bon ordre.***

1. Those are the chocolates / loves / my mother / that .
2. what / Do you know / wants / your father ?
3. You made / cry / my sister .
4. starts / what time / the match / Did you ask ?
5. I don't understand / makes / the decisions / that / the government .
6. lives / where / the Smith family / Can you tell me ?
7. two men and a woman with a baby / We saw / the car / get into .
8. I didn't hear / drive away / the car .
9. where / my father / That's the office / works .
10. the rain / Don't let / get in !
11. Perhaps / not too late / is / it .

PRÉPOSITIONS : EN FIN DE GROUPE VERBAL *(AZ 306)*

**9. *Les éléments des phrases suivantes ont été mélangés. Remettez-les dans le bon ordre.***

1. of / did / What / die / last year / your friend ?
2. you / Here's / were looking / for / the photo .
3. to live / a very interesting town / in / It's not .
4. likes / at / No one / being laughed .
5. from / the illness / my mum / suffered / That's / all her life.
6. all this time / have / Who / they / for / been waiting ?
7. to worry / about / nothing / There's .
8. already / of / been taken care / This problem / has .

EXERCICE DE SYNTHÈSE

**10. *Trouvez l'erreur dans chaque phrase et corrigez-la. (Il s'agit le plus souvent d'une erreur dans l'ordre des mots.)***

1. We go seldom to the cinema. *(AZ 290)*
2. He hardly is twelve years old. *(AZ 290)*
3. You all have had your difficulties. *(AZ 290)*
4. They did even not phone us! *(AZ 290)*
5. You don't certainly do it that way. *(AZ 290)*
6. She's perhaps not interested in rugby. *(AZ 291)*

→

7. I don't speak very well French. *(AZ 292)*
8. We used to enjoy a lot dancing. *(AZ 292)*
9. You spoke yesterday very passionately at the meeting. *(AZ 293)*
10. She's not enough strong to carry it. *(AZ 126)*
11. Have we got enough of ice cream? *(AZ 126)*
12. The half of my books were stolen. *(AZ 165)*
13. See you in a half hour! *(AZ 165)*
14. That's a quite interesting opinion. *(AZ 342)*
15. We like rather jazz. *(AZ 343)*
16. It's a such wonderful restaurant. *(AZ 362)*
17. You're a girl so nice! *(AZ 362)*
18. Take off them immediately! *(AZ 398)*
19. Explain me the rules, will you? *(AZ 396)*
20. Not only I had forgotten their address, but … *(AZ 207)*
21. Ask her what does she want. *(AZ 208)*
22. This is the poem that wrote Tom. *(AZ 208)*
23. Did you hear speak someone? *(AZ 208)*
24. From where did your father come? *(AZ 306)*

# 27 Les prépositions

PRÉPOSITIONS : APRÈS UN VERBE … ; **MARRY … ; HEAR FROM …** *(AZ 304, 229, 174)*

***1. Complétez par la préposition qui convient ou par Ø.***

1. You've been very kind ..... everyone.
2. I'm looking .... my hat. Have you seen it anywhere?
3. 'Has he heard ..... Judy?' 'Not a word.'
4. We succeeded ..... persuading him to join us.
5. Please forgive ..... them!
6. It's a painting ..... Matisse.
7. Can you account ..... your absence on Monday?
8. We were disappointed ..... the results.
9. They're going to be late ..... the concert.
10. We've just heard ..... his operation. Is he OK?
11. I have to translate this ..... Arabic.
12. He married ..... her in May. She divorced ..... him in June.
13. I've been thinking ..... this problem for a long time.
14. What is it made .....?
15. She borrowed £10 ..... me last week.
16. I'd like to discuss ..... this question with you.
17. Hurry up and get ..... the bus!
18. What did you see when you entered ..... the room?
19. I can't believe that you've never heard ..... Gandhi!
20. She's always laughing ..... other people.

PRÉPOSITIONS : EN DÉBUT D'EXPRESSION *(AZ 305)*

***2. Complétez par la préposition qui convient.***

1. ..... my opinion we should go ..... strike!
2. 'Who was ..... the phone?' 'Joe.' 'Isn't he ..... duty today?'
3. The house ..... the other side of the street was ..... fire.
4. ..... the end we went ..... train.
5. There's never anything good ..... TV ..... the morning.
6. 'Come ..... night,' she said ..... a quiet voice.

**AT, IN, ON, TO, INTO, ONTO** *(AZ 52-54, 191)*

***3. Mettez*** at, in, on, to, into, onto ***ou* Ø.**

1. 'Is Sue ..... home?' 'I'm afraid she's ..... hospital. She had an accident on the way ..... school – ..... just a mile from here!'
2. 'What can you see ..... the photo?' 'There's a man ..... glasses. He's ..... prison. He's going ..... his cell.'
3. 'Lets go away ..... the weekend.' 'Sorry, I'm playing football ..... Saturday.'
4. 'They're going skiing ..... Chamonix ..... March.' 'Really? We went ..... Chamonix .....1992.'
5. We're going out ..... dinner ..... Cathy and Tim's. We should arrive ..... home before midnight.
6. 'When did you arrive ..... Thailand?' '..... May 16th.'
7. Did they take you ..... the police station?
8. Throw it ..... me – gently *(= doucement)*!
9. They kept shooting ..... us even after the cease-fire!
10. 'Are you going ..... home?' 'No, I'm going ..... the doctor's.'
11. When I went back ..... the room, she was still ..... the telephone.
12. As soon as he saw the rat he jumped ..... the table.

**ABOUT ; APRÈS ; AVANT ; BY (THE TIME)** *(AZ 1, 2, 37, 58, 71)*

***4. Traduisez les mots en italique.***

1. Nous sommes désolés *pour* le bruit.
2. Ils étaient à l'école ensemble, mais *après* ils se sont perdus de vue.
3. "Ça prendra combien de temps?" "*Dix jours environ.*"
4. Moi, je suis d'accord, mais il faudra que j'en parle avec ma femme *avant.*
5. Elle pensait *à* sa mère.
6. Peux-tu me le rendre *au plus tard à la fin de la semaine*?
7. Il a fait un discours intéressant *sur* l'art moderne.
8. *D'ici à ce qu'elle me téléphone*, je serai de retour.
9. *Et si on allait* à Rome?
10. À qui as-tu parlé *après*?

**ACCORDING TO** ; CHEZ ; EN FACE DE ; **FROM** ; JUSQU'À
*(AZ 5, 79, 122, 147, 213)*
***5. Traduisez les mots en italique.***

1. *D'après son médecin*, l'opération est sans danger.
2. Il doit travailler *jusqu'à 80 heures par semaine*!
3. Qui était l'homme *en face de vous* au dîner ce soir?
4. Je serai au bureau *de 9 heures à 11 heures.*
5. *Pour moi*, ils devraient se marier.
6. Il habite toujours *chez ses parents.*
7. On n'a pas le droit de stationner *devant la maison.*
8. *À partir de demain* je ne fumerai plus!
9. Avec ce nouveau télescope on pourra voir *jusqu'aux limites de l'univers (= the edge of the universe).*
10. "Où est Simone?" *"Elle est rentrée chez elle."*
11. Voulez-vous lire *jusqu'à la fin du premier paragraphe*?
12. Ils ont volé de l'argent *à une vieille dame.*
13. Il y a beaucoup de passion *chez Racine.*
14. Mon permis me donne le droit de conduire *jusqu'à l'âge de 70 ans.*

**ACROSS ...** ; DEVANT ; **DURING** ET **FOR** ; **DURING** ET **WHILE** ; **FOR** (BUT) *(AZ 6, 101, 111, 112, 142)*
***6. Choisissez la préposition qui convient.***

1. They plan to walk *across/ through* the Antarctic.
2. In this photo Tom is standing *before/ in front of* Joe.
3. Let's go out *during/ while* the sun is shining.
4. He got in *across/ through* the bathroom window.
5. We're going skiing *for/ during* two weeks in March.
6. He had to appear *before/ in front of* a military tribunal.
7. She's gone to the airport *for/ to* meet her mother.

## 28 Les mots de liaison

MOTS DE LIAISON *(AZ 240)*

***1. Retrouvez l'équivalent anglais des mots de liaison suivants.***

| |
|---|
| au contraire   au fait   au moins   autrement dit   bref<br>d'ailleurs   d'après moi   d'après Paul   d'un autre côté<br>d'un côté   dans l'ensemble   en fait   en tout cas<br>pour moi   pourtant   quant à Paul   remarque   sinon<br>tout de même |

| |
|---|
| on the other hand   by the way   actually   on the whole<br>according to Paul   in my opinion   yet   anyway<br>on the contrary   at least   besides   I think<br>all the same   in other words   in a word   mind you<br>otherwise   as for Paul   in a way |

**ALSO** ET **SO** ; **AS** ET **LIKE** ; **EITHER … OR** ; **NOT EITHER** ; **BOTH**
*(AZ 26, 45, 117, 118, 67)*

***2. Complétez par*** also, so, as, like, either, neither ***et*** both.

1. I once worked ..... a secretary when I was a student.
2. ..... we go now or we stay at home.
3. They were in a hurry, ..... they took a taxi.
4. She's got ..... the time nor the money to do this.
5. ..... I told you yesterday, I have made my decision.
6. His job is ..... boring and badly-paid.
7. 'She doesn't understand computers.' 'He doesn't .....'
8. In Ireland ..... in England the weather is often cold and wet.
9. I speak ..... French and German.
10. You're ..... my father: he worries a lot too.
11. ..... my sister nor my brother eat meat.
12. They live in New York, but they've ..... got a house in London.

EVER : SES COMPOSÉS *(AZ 131)*

***3. Complétez en utilisant des composés de* ever.**

1. You can do ..... you like. It's all the same to me!
2. ..... she watches this film, she always wants to cry.
3. 'Tea or coffee?' 'I don't mind. ..... is easier.'
4. ..... clearly we explain it to them, they never understand.
5. Give it to ..... wants it.
6. That picture looks horrible ..... you put it.
7. We always lose ..... well we play against them.
8. ..... the weather is like, he always goes out for a walk every day.
9. The police will find him ..... he's hiding.
10. ..... did this must be mad!
11. I feel sad ..... you go away.
12. You can take either the nine o'clock train or the ten o'clock. ..... one you take, you'll easily arrive in time for your meeting.

## 29 Comment traduire ...?

IL FAUT ; MANQUER ; PLAIRE *(AZ 188, 228, 294)*

***1. Traduisez en anglais.***

1. Il faut que j'écrive à ma mère ce soir.
2. Il nous faudra encore six chaises *(= six more ...)*.
3. Il faut que tu viennes à l'heure *(= on time)*!
4. Il a fallu dix ans pour le construire. (prétérit)
5. Il faudra deux jours pour finir ce travail.
6. Ce livre manque d'intérêt. (= Il n'en a pas assez.)
7. Il leur manque l'argent nécessaire. (= Ils ne l'ont pas.)
8. Mes parents m'ont beaucoup manqué. (prétérit)
9. Dépêche-toi! Tu vas rater l'autobus!
10. Cet hôtel vous plaira, je crois.
11. Est-ce que nous leur avons plu? (prétérit)
12. Le concert ne m'a pas plu du tout.

IL Y A *(AZ 189, 18, 332)*

***2. Traduisez en anglais.***

1. Il y a deux solutions à *(= to)* ce problème.
2. Ils se sont mariés *(= got married)* il y a dix ans.
3. Il y a six semaines qu'elle ne m'a écrit.
4. J'ai arrêté de fumer il y a longtemps.
5. Il y a longtemps qu'elle habite à Paris.
6. Il y a ton père qui te cherche.
7. Il y avait un homme qui me regardait.
8. Il y a quelqu'un qui a oublié une chaussure.
9. Il y a des élèves *(= schoolchildren)* qui sont très difficiles.
10. Il y a beaucoup de morts sur les routes *(= the roads)* chaque année. *(AZ 98.4)*

FAIRE FAIRE *(AZ 136)*

***3. Traduisez en anglais.***

1. Mon mari me fait conduire très lentement.
2. Fais-leur se laver les mains *(= their hands)*!
3. Ne la faites pas pleurer.
4. Ils font nettoyer les tapis *(= carpets)* tous les ans.
5. Il faut que vous fassiez remplacer le pneu *(= tyre)*.
6. Elle s'est fait couper les cheveux. (present perfect)
7. Nous allons faire installer *(= instal)* le chauffage central *(= central heating)*.
8. Je fais faire la vaisselle *(= the washing-up)* à mes enfants.
9. Nos parents nous faisaient lever de très bonne heure.
10. Je me fais construire une petite maison à la campagne.

EN + PARTICIPE PRÉSENT *(AZ 120)*

***4. Traduisez en anglais.***

1. "Je vais les tuer!" dit Sophie en prenant *(= pick up)* un grand couteau.
2. En attendant à l'arrêt de l'autobus, Pierre a été témoin *(= witnessed)* d'un accident de voiture.
3. En ouvrant la porte, elle a reconnu l'homme tout de suite. (prétérit)
4. En faisant la cuisine *(= to cook)*, il s'est brûlé le doigt *(= burned his finger)*.

5. "Comment puis-je la persuader de rester?" "En lui demandant de te pardonner *(= forgive).*"
6. Il a monté l'escalier *(= ... upstairs)* en courant. (prétérit)
7. "Ne me quittez pas," dit-elle en pleurant.
8. En le présentant *(= introduce)*, j'ai oublié son nom!
9. En travaillant dur, vous réussirez *(= pass)* vos examens.
10. En allant au bureau, ma mère a laissé tomber *(= dropped)* son parapluie.

## 30 La grammaire des mots

**(I) WISH** *(AZ 411)*

***1. Transformez les phrases à l'aide de*** wish ***ou*** hope ***en faisant les autres changements nécessaires.***

**Ex. :** I'm not very tall. *I wish I was taller.*

1. He hasn't got a car.
2. I have to go to work everyday.
3. We got married when we were teenagers.
4. She spent all her money on new clothes.
5. Hurry up, will you? (It's getting late!)
6. Write to me more often!
7. You might visit us again next year.
8. I might have some time tomorrow.
9. They live in the city.
10. I didn't go to university.
11. Stop criticising my work!
12. He might telephone me at the weekend.

**GET** *(AZ 157-159)*

***2. Traduisez en anglais en utilisant les structures avec*** get.

1. Commandons encore une bouteille de vin!
2. Lève-toi! Tu vas être en retard!
3. Je me fatiguais et je commençais à avoir faim.
4. Ils se sont perdus dans la neige. (prétérit)
5. Quand est-ce que vous avez divorcé? (prétérit)

→

6. Heureusement *(= Fortunately)*, personne n'a été tué. (prétérit)
7. Il a essayé de les faire se presser. (prétérit)
8. Je n'arrive pas à faire comprendre ça à mon mari.
9. Elle n'a pas réussi à faire démarrer la voiture. (prétérit)

**AGREE ; ASK ; EXPLAIN ; SUGGEST ; THINK ; WANT**

*(AZ 19, 50, 134, 373, 384, 402)*

***3. Traduisez en anglais.***

1. Nous n'étions pas d'accord avec leur décision.
2. Il m'a demandé ma nationalité. (prétérit)
3. Demande la clef à Paul, et demande-lui le chemin de *(= the way to)* la maison.
4. Avez-vous expliqué la situation aux enfants?
5. Je t'expliquerai ce que tu dois faire.
6. Il nous a suggéré une autre date. (prétérit)
7. Peux-tu proposer à Ann de venir mardi soir?
8. Je leur ai suggéré de passer l'examen *(= take the exam)* l'année prochaine.
9. Nous proposons d'y aller en autobus.
10. Je pense souvent à mes vacances.
11. Qu'est-ce que tu penses de cette musique?
12. Il pensait la trouver au bureau, mais elle était déjà partie.
13. Ils pensent qu'ils n'auront pas assez de temps pour le faire.
14. Je pense inviter Richard à dîner ce week-end.
15. Pourquoi veux-tu apprendre l'anglais?
16. Ses parents veulent qu'il devienne médecin, mais il ne veut pas.
17. Elle voudrait trouver un travail, mais son mari ne veut pas. Il veut qu'elle reste à la maison avec les enfants.
18. "Je peux laisser les documents ici?" "Comme vous voulez."

# 31 Mots à ne pas confondre

***Êtes-vous sûr de savoir bien employer ces mots? Complétez les phrases, puis vérifiez vos réponses dans le corrigé. (Les renvois s'y trouvent.)***

1. Shut up and ..... me, will you! *(hear/ listen)*
2. 'Where's Paul?' 'I think he's ..... in the bath!' *(always/ still)*
3. 'Do you think Ann's as clever ..... her sister?' 'No, Sara's cleverer ..... Ann.' *(as/ than)*
4. I ..... live in a big house. Now I ..... living in this little flat. *('m used to/ used to)*
5. 'She .....?!' 'Yes, she ..... in her sleep.' *(be dead/ die)*
6. Do you know the name of the .....? *(dead/ dead man)*
7. How many people ..... in the explosion yesterday? *(be dead/ die)*
8. '.....'s work?' 'OK.' 'And .....'s your new boss like?' 'No idea. I don't even know ..... she looks like.' *(how/ what)*
9. 'Extension 412.' 'Can I speak to Tony, please?' 'Sorry, he's not ..... at the moment.' *(here/ there)*
10. Could you ..... me of his name? *(remember/ remind)*
11. Have a nice .....! *(journey/ travel)*
12. 'When will you get back from your .....?' 'Tomorrow evening.' *(trip/ voyage)*
13. How did you ..... when you ..... off the roof? *(fall/ feel)*
14. She'll never ..... me. We're going to ..... together for ever! *(leave/ live)*
15. 'It's very ..... here.' 'Yes, it's ..... nice.' *(quiet/ quite)*
16. The ..... situation isn't getting any better, is it? *(economic/ economical)*
17. Did you ..... me to come? *(expect/ wait)*
18. ..... this to the post office for me, will you? *(bring/ take)*

A à Z

# Corrigés

• Dans ces corrigés, les formes verbales qui peuvent être contractées le sont généralement.
La forme non contractée est également possible dans la plupart des cas.
• Sont données entre parenthèses des solutions correctes mais peu employées.
• Certains exercices sont divergents. Leur corrigé suggère des réponses possibles.

## 1 Déterminants : articles

***1 /*** *a*: beautiful overcoat, great honour, headache, hospital, student, uniform
*an*: easy question, honest man, hour, invitation, opinion, unusual name
*Ø*: excellent Chinese, heavy rain, icy water, information, machines, new furniture, stupidity

***2 /*** 1. *an* architect 2. *a* job
5. *a* teacher 6. *an* interesting job
7. *a* long journey 8. *a* pity
10. *a* sense of humour

***3 /*** 1. ~~the~~ love 3. ~~The~~ violence … ~~the~~ modern society 4. on ~~the~~ TV
6. ~~The~~ inflation 8. ~~The~~ Irish coffee … ~~the~~ Irish whiskey *(Les autres phrases sont correctes.)*

***4 /*** *Vous n'aurez besoin de* the *que dans les phrases suivantes.*
3. According to *the* latest forecast … *the* next five days
6. … learning (Ø) Dutch … speaks (Ø) English in *the* Netherlands
9. *the* latest Roddy Doyle novel … *the* last one 11. *the* last two nights

***5 /*** 1. Ø 2. Ø 3. an 4. Ø 5. Ø 6. Ø 7. an 8. The 9. The 10. a 11. a 12. Ø 13. Ø 14. Ø 15. The 16. Ø 17. Ø 18. Ø 19. the 20. the 21. a 22. the 23. the 24. the 25. the

## 2 Déterminants : *all, both, some, …*

***1 /*** 1. Every / Each 2. all
3. every / each 4. each / every
5. each / (every) 6. all 7. Each / (Every) 8. each 9. Every
10. each 11. Every 12. each

***2 /*** 1. all; everything; whole; whole; everything
2. whole; All; whole; whole
3. all / the whole; whole; whole; all; everything

***3 /*** 1. Both the doors were locked.
2. She was in love with both men.
3. Niamh and Donal / Donal and Niamh are both Irish names.
4. Both my grandfather and my grandmother / Both my grandmother and my grandfather came from Russia. 5. He both plays the piano and sings / sings and plays the piano. 6. This flat is both spacious and inexpensive / inexpensive and spacious 7. Both of them live in Canada. 8. I enjoy both modern music and classical music / classical music and modern music.

***4 /*** 1. She doesn't want either of them. 2. Neither of us can speak

Spanish. 3. We can't come either weekend. 4. Neither of my sisters likes jazz. 5. Neither of my parents eats meat. 6. We could go to either country.

***5/*** 1. any; any; some; some; some 2. any; any; any; any; some/any; any 3. any 4. Ø 5. Ø; Ø

***6/*** 2. Both ~~of~~ men 6. Some ~~of~~ modern art

***7/*** 1. There aren't any new students./ There are no new students. 2. She doesn't want any more soup./ She wants no more soup. 3. He hasn't got a car./ He's got no car. 4. None of us knows how to ski. 5. They haven't got any children./ They've got no children. 6. None of these people can speak Arabic. 7. There isn't any cheese in the fridge./ There's no cheese in the fridge. 8. I didn't have a headache./ I had no headache. *(AZ 170)* 9. We haven't got any time left. / We've got no time left.

***8/*** 1. Anybody 2. anything 3. Any 4. Anywhere 5. anything 6. any 7. anybody 8. anywhere

***9/*** 1. someone/ somebody 2. everyone/ everybody 3. anywhere; anyone/ anybody 4. Nowhere 5. No one/ Nobody; anything 6. anything; nothing; something; somewhere 7. anyone/ anybody; no one/ nobody; something; everything; nothing; Something

***10/*** 1. ... all day. 2. Every time ... 3. Not everybody is/ Everybody isn't as generous ... 4. ... every day. 5. ... on each foot. 6. ... we gave our children everything!
7. ... a whole month. 8. ... both play football. 9. ... speak both Spanish and French.
10. ... Neither, thanks ...
11. Our teacher didn't accept either/ accepted neither of ...
12. ... haven't got any time.
13. ... put some milk ...
14. He's got very long fingers.
15. She hasn't got a cat.
16. ...visit us any day ...
17. ... at any moment.
18. Everybody is waiting.
19. We've never travelled anywhere/We've travelled nowhere ...

## 3 Déterminants : *little, few, much, ...*

***1/*** 1. A little wine, madam? 2. She's had a few problems with her husband. 3. I've seen her a few times. We've spent some time together. 4. They've been a little/ bit stupid. 5. We'll need quite a lot / bit of money. 6. 'Do you have many students?' 'Yes, quite a few.' 7. Few parents/ Not many parents understand their children. 8. We have very little time left.

***2/*** 1. many 2. much 3. much 4. many 5. much 6. a lot of/ lots of/ (many) 7. much 8. many 9. a lot 10. A lot of/ Lots of 11. A lot of/ Lots of 12. a lot

***3/*** 1. How much 2. so many 3. too much 4. so much 5. How many 6. too much 7. How much 8. So much 9. Too many 10. How many

***4/*** 1. too 2. enough 3. too many 4. enough 5. enough of 6. enough 7. too much of 8. too much 9. enough 10. too 11. too many of

***5/*** 1. other 2. another 3. others 4. other 5. another 6. another 7. others 8. other

***6/*** 2. ... much ~~of~~ petrol left.
4. Many ~~of~~ people ...
5. ... enough ~~of~~ meat? 7. ... too much ~~of~~ difficulty ... 9. Most ~~of~~ homes ... 10. Most ~~of~~ people ...

## 4 Démonstratifs et possessifs

***1/*** 1. that 2. this 3. those 4. these 5. That 6. these 7. this 8. those 9. that 10. these

***2/*** 1. Her 2. our 3. your; hers 4. Mine; Theirs 5. one's 6. my 7. his 8. your books 9. his 10. your mother's

***3/*** 1. dog's 2. Joe's and Sue's 3. Jones' 4. Ann's 5. Young children's' 6. President of Ireland's 7. men's 8. dentist's 9. Saturday's 10. students'/ young children's 11. old woman's/ dentist's/ President of Ireland's

***4/*** 1. Those are Veronica's CDs. 2. ... the women's representative? 3. I'm the Head of Department's secretary. 4. These are Paul's and Sarah's toothbrushes. 5. ... Alan's. 6. ... at the doctor's ... 7. ... Mike and Linda's ... 8. He broke the back of the chair. 9. It was a play by Shakespeare. 10. That's the mother of the baby that was kidnapped. 11. ... the Matisse exhibition?

## 5 Mots interrogatifs

***1/*** 1. What 2. which 3. Which 4. What (Which) 5. What 6. Which

***2/*** 1. Whose bicycle is that? Whose is that bicycle? 2. Whose books are those? Whose are those books? 3. Whose house is this? Whose is this house? 4. Whose children are these? Whose are these children? 5. Whose dog is it? 6. Whose wedding are you going to?

***3/*** 1. Who lives in that house? 2. Who did you speak to? *(AZ 306.1)* 3. Who were they with? 4. Who did you see? 5. Who has just got married? 6. Who don't you like? 7. Who did they give the money to? 8. Who is she standing in front of?

## 6 Les noms

***1/*** car**s** : baths, birds, chairs, chiefs, flats, grown-ups, houses, keys, (persons), roofs, socks, toys
bus**es** : boxes, brushes, glasses, potatoes, watches
bab**ies** : countries, factories
hal**ves** : knives, wives
Autre forme : children, crises, data, fish, feet, passers-by, pence, people, phenomena, sheep, teeth, women judges

***2/*** 1. their 2. Ø 3. is 4. Ø 5. a 6. a piece of 7. are 8. Ø 9. is 10. has 11. is 12. This; is 13. were 14. hasn't

***3/*** *(Voici les combinaisons les plus courantes.)*
art gallery/programme(s)/shop(s)
business office(s)/paper(s)/ programme(s) *et* businessman (businessmen)
fish market(s)/shop(s)
jeans market(s)/shop(s)
living-room(s)
news programme(s) *et* newspaper(s)
police station(s) *et* policeman (policemen)
sports bag(s)/programme(s)/ shop(s) *et* sportsman (sportsmen)
tennis match(es)
three-day journey(s)
ticket office(s)
timetable(s)
toilet paper *(indénombrable, donc pas de pluriel)*
traffic light(s)
woman astronaut (women astronauts)

## 7 Les pronoms

***1/*** 1. one 2. ones 3. Ø 4. ones 5. Ø 6. one 7. one

***2/*** 1. My friend works in a factory. 2. Joe and Tom are brothers. 3. The subject that he enjoys least is mathematics. 4. Don't worry – we'll do it! 5. My boyfriend and I are getting married. 6. They live in a house. I live in a flat. 7. Shall I turn it off ? 8. Can you describe the man to me? 9. Tell Brigit that lunch is ready. 10. Jack is still too young to dress himself.

**3/** 1. myself 2. herself 3. each other / one another 4. oneself 5. each other / one another 6. ourselves 7. themselves 8. each other's / one another's 9. himself 10. each other / one another

**4/** 1. It 2. She 3. He 4. It 5. That 6. It 7. She 8. It

**5/** 1. themselves 2. their 3. they 4. them 5. they 6. themselves 7. them 8. their

**6/** 1. You / One can't always be right. 2. In Austria they / people speak German. 3. We / People express it in a different way in French. 4. Where are we going / shall we go this evening? 5. You never have / One never has enough time in life to do everything. 6. We arrived very late. 7. In Paris people / they / we are always in a hurry. 8. They / People don't play football a lot in the USA.

**7/** 1. My telephone number has been changed. 2. Someone / Somebody is waiting for you downstairs. A gentleman …
3. The house was built thirty years ago. 4. Paul! Someone / Somebody is calling you! 5. The money will be sent to you. / You'll be sent the money. 6. My bag has been stolen! / Someone / Somebody has stolen my bag!
7. Someone / Somebody has sent me some flowers!

**8/** 1. who / that 2. which / that 3. that / Ø 4. that 5. who / that / Ø 6. that / (which) 7. which / that / Ø 8. that / Ø 9. that

**9/** 1. What 2. which 3. that 4. which 5. what 6. that 7. which 8. What 9. that

**10/** 1. … whose name I can never remember. 2. … woman whose husband left her? 3. It's a job the value of which / whose value is often underestimated.
4. … a person Ø / whom/that everyone was jealous of. 5. It's dogs Ø / which / that he's afraid of.
6. He's a man Ø / whom / that you need to be careful of.
7. … children, two of whom …
8. … novels, the most famous of which are …

**11/** 1. She's the woman (who / that) we work for. 2. Are these the books (which / that) he is interested in? 3. This is the family (who / that) I stayed with. 4. Here's the hole (which / that) the rat came out of. 5. He's the man (who / that) she's getting married to. 6. This is the problem (which / that) they are worried about. 7. They are the people (who / that) we are playing against.

**12/** 2. The journey, which was very uncomfortable, lasted ten hours. 3. The people who / that live downstairs are French.
4. My brother, who has a house in Cambridge, works in London.
6. The car which / that is outside belongs to my neighbour. 7. Tom, who / whom you met last night, is moving to the USA next month.

## 8 Les adjectifs

**1/** 1. … a very exciting story.
2. … very difficult.
3. …the vegetable market?
4. I was worried and I asked …
5. … your white cotton dress?
6. … an expensive leather jacket.
7. … a famous American film star?
8. … beautiful black hair.
9. The last two days …
10. … a long, heavy coat.
11. … that aluminium and glass table? 12. … young, rich and good-looking.

**2/** 1. He likes open-minded people. 2. I asked a friendly-looking policeman. 3. She is very good-natured. 4. … towards the stone-throwing crowd. 5. … 'Blue-green.' 6. I'm right-handed.
7. … a plant-eating animal.

**3/** 1. 'He's lost his wife.' 'The poor man! / Poor man!' 2. We work a lot with the handicapped / with handicapped people. 3. The important thing is to have a good time! 4. The rich/ Rich people have to pay more taxes than the poor/ than poor people. 5. A blind man/ person was attacked yesterday by two young men/ young people/ youths. 6. It is said that the Irish are very musical. 7. She's got a Japanese woman and six French people in her English class. 8. The government is not very interested in the unemployed/ in unemployed people. 9. What are the main needs of the mentally il/ of mentally ill people? 10. I don't like selfish people.

## 9 La comparaison

***1/*** 1. older; noisier 2. easier; easiest 3. latest 4. biggest 5. happiest 6. more intelligent 7. most expensive 8. harder 9. worst 10. more 11. elder; older; younger; eldest 12. more carefully; faster; most slowly 13. earlier; earliest; farthest/ furthest 14. more; less; least; further 15. further/ farther 16. better; worse; best

***2/*** 1. Joe is much/ far/ a lot more intelligent than Alan. 2. This question is much/ far/ a lot easier than the first question. 3. She is much/ far/ a lot younger than him/ he is. 4. Mary drives much/ far/ a lot faster than me/ I do. 5. Bob is much/ far/ a lot fatter than you/ you are. 6. You sing even better than her/ she does. 7. We work even quicker/ more quickly than they do.

***3/*** 1. worse and worse 2. more and more 3. The fatter ... the happier 4. less and less 5. the more pleased 6. more and more expensive 7. The less ... the less 8. the better 9. The more ... the less 10. more and more popular.

***4/*** 1. the 2. Ø/ the 3. the 4. Ø 5. Ø 6. the; in 7. the 8. the; of 9. more/ (most) 10. younger; older 11. stronger; weaker; best

***5/*** 1. South America is twice as big as Europe. 2. I don't speak French as well as you/ you do. 3. London is as interesting as Paris. 4. I don't drink as much beer as him/ he does. 5. There are five times as many people in China as in the USA. 6. There isn't as much oil in Mexico as in Saudi Arabia.

***6/*** 1. as; as; less; than 2. least 3. as little 4. less; fewer/ less; than 5. as few 6. least 7. fewest/ least 8. at least 9. least 10. at least

***7/*** 1. They need as much money as possible. 2. It's the most pleasant bar in the town. 3. Please send us further information. 4. 'He played/ has played much (far/ a lot) worse than you/ you did/ you have.' 'So much the better/ All the better.' 5. My elder brother is about to get married. 6. The weather is/ It's even colder today than yesterday. 7. It's the worst match of the season. 8. She's getting weaker and weaker. 9. The more money they earn, the less happy they are. 10. I'm all the sorrier / more sorry because/as/since I didn't write / haven't written to you. 11. The weather is coldest in January. 12. He doesn't dance as well as you / you do.

## 10 *Be, have* et *do*

***1/*** 1. Are 2. were 3. isn't 4. be 5. don't be 6. aren't 7. 's/ 's being 8. 're being 9. Wasn't 10. 's *(= has)* been 11. would have been

***2/*** 1. 's/ 's got 2. is/ 's 3. hasn't 4. Were 5. 'm not 6. Have 7. 're 8. 's *(= has)* 9. 's *(= is)* 10. have/ 've got 11. was 12. 's *(= has)*

***3/*** 1. We've *got* three children. 3. They haven't *got* any money.

5. Have you *got* the time, please? 6. She's *got* red hair. 8. I haven't *got* a particular opinion on this matter.

***4 /*** 1. had a wonderful dream 2. have a try 3. have a nice time 4. 's having a shower 5. Did you have lunch; had a cup of coffee 6. 'll have a nervous breakdown 7. have a swim 8. have a look at 9. don't you have a rest 10. had a terrible holiday

***5 /*** 1. She does want to meet you! 2. Do stop doing that! 3. ... 'Yes, do.' 4. ... But he does eat fish. 5. ... 'I did tell her.' 6. ... 'They did finish the job – two weeks ago.' 7. ... and she did forget. 8. ... he did move to London.

***6 /*** 1. ... 'We do.' 2. ... the year before my dad did. 3. ... and Sue does too. 4. ... more than I do. 5. ... 'Yes, he does.' 6. ... 'We did as well.' 7. ... 'Really? I always do.' 8. ... until Alison did. 9. ... better than my sister does.

***7 /*** *do :* a big favour, a lot of harm, her hair, her homework, his duty, some work, something stupid, the cleaning, your best

*make :* a terrible fuss, all the arrangements, an attempt, enquiries, her wedding dress, peace, the beds, too many mistakes, too much noise

## 11 Modaux : *can, could, may* et *might*

***1 /*** 1. can / could / may 2. can't / cannot / may not; isn't allowed 3. can / could / may / (might) 4. May / Might 5. wasn't allowed 6. can / may 7. could / might 8. may / can 9. aren't allowed 10. isn't allowed

***2 /*** 1. When she was a year old, she could walk but she couldn't run. 2. When she was two years old, she could use a knife and fork but she couldn't dress herself. 3. When she was three years old, she couldn't count from 1 to 10 but she could draw pictures. 4. When she was four years old, she could say the alphabet and (she could) write her name. 5. When she was five years old, she could read but she couldn't tell the time. 6. Now that she is six years old, she can't programme the video but she can play with the computer.

***3 /*** 1. can 2. can't 3. could 4. couldn't 5. could 6. can / 'm able to 7. be able to 8. will be able to 9. been able to 10. being able to 11. cannot / is unable to

***4 /*** 1. ... was able to / managed to find ... 3. ... I was able to / managed to get to sleep ... 5. ... we were able to / managed to finish ... 7. The police were able to / managed to catch ...
*(Could peut être remplacé par* was able to *ou* managed to *dans les autres phrases, mais ce n'est pas obligatoire.)*

***5 /*** 1. may / might 2. might / may 3. might 4. might 5. might / may 6. might / may 7. might 8. might 9. might 10. may / might

***6 /*** 1. could / might have become 2. can have happened; can't have disappeared 3. could have killed 4. could / might have told; might / could have said 5. may / might have been; could / might have started; could / might have been

***7 /*** 1. Could / May / Can / (Might) 2. Can / Could 3. might / (could) 4. be able to 5. isn't allowed 6. can't / cannot; can 7. might / (could) 8. could / might 9. can't 10. couldn't 11. might 12. won't be allowed to 13. managed to 14. could / might 15. 'll be able to

## 12 Modaux : *must, have to, need, should* et *ought*

***1 /*** 1. must 2. Does ... have to 3. had to 4. must 5. don't have to 6. must 7. won't have to 8. mustn't 9. haven't had to 10. have to 11. had to / must 12. 'll have to

***2 /*** 1. Do you need 2. to buy 3. wait 4. to phone 5. to say 6. needn't / don't need to 7. doesn't need 8. have come 9. painting 10. don't need to

***3 /*** 1. must have forgotten 2. can't have gone 3. had to go 4. can't have seen 5. had to stay 6. must have had 7. must have eaten 8. had to buy 9. had to work 10. can't have got 11. must have taken

***4 /*** 1. The nations of the world must learn ... 2. Maybe we should buy ... 3. They must come ... 4. Perhaps they shouldn't get married. 5. It should be finished ... 6. It must arrive ... 7. We mustn't stop ... 8. This job shouldn't be ...

***5 /*** 1. ... you ought to become ... 2. You oughtn't to eat ... 3. Ought I to take ... 4. Paul ought to beat ... 5. She oughtn't to take ... 6. Ought we to clean ...

***6 /*** 1. I shouldn't have got up late. / ... I oughtn't to have got up ... 2. I should have caught the bus. / ... I ought to have caught ... 3. I should have been more careful. / ... I ought to have been ... 4. I should have remembered our meeting. / ... I ought to have remembered ... 5. I shouldn't have eaten so much for lunch. / ... I oughtn't to have eaten ... 6. I should have worked more quickly. / ... I ought to have worked ... 7. I shouldn't have forgotten to phone her. / ... I oughtn't to have forgotten ... 8. I should have stayed in bed. / ... I ought to have stayed ...

***7 /*** 1. I mustn't lose the key. 2. When I was a child I had to go to bed at nine (o'clock). 3. You/We should / ought to / must think of others. 4. They were supposed to / were to get married, but ... 5. You should / ought to ring Paul. 6. He was to become a famous writer. 7. I'm seeing / I'm supposed to see them tomorrow. 8. If they left London, she would have to look for a new job. 9. Eleven o'clock: she really must be at her office now.

***8 /*** 1. (Elle) devait 2. (Il) doit 3. (Ils) ne doivent pas 4. (Tu) ne devrais pas / (Vous) devriez pas 5. (Nous) devions 6. doivent / devraient 7. (Je) devais (les retrouver) 8. (Nous) devons 9. (Je) devrais 10. (Tu) devrais / (Vous) devriez 11. (Je) devais 12. (Ils) doivent

***9 /*** 1. have (got) to / must 2. should / ought to 3. 'll have to / 'll need to 4. needn't / doesn't need to / doesn't have to 5. must 6. to have to 7. needs 8. must / have (got) to 9. shouldn't / oughtn't to 10. need to / 've got to / have to 11. shouldn't / oughtn't to 12. don't have to / don't need to / needn't

***10 /*** 1. should / ought to have remembered 2. must have forgotten 3. shouldn't / oughtn't to have told 4. must have left 5. should / ought to have written

## 13 La modalité : autres usages

***1 /*** 1. You'd better take an aspirin / not go to work. 2. You'd better not wake him/her up. 3. You'd better call the police. 4. You'd better not light a cigarette. 5. You'd better have a haircut. 6. You'd better not eat it. 7. You'd better clean them. 8. You'd better not forget it. 9. You'd better take some exercise. 10. You'd better not play football.

***2 /*** *(Phrases suggérées)*
1. 'm supposed to be in Cambridge at five o'clock 2. 's supposed to be very charming 3. was supposed to meet him 4. 's not / isn't supposed to eat meat 5. were supposed to get them from Ann 6. 're not / aren't supposed to smoke in here 7. was supposed to come by plane 8. 're supposed to wear these on your head 9. were supposed to play the match

***3/*** 1. used to/ would 2. used to 3. didn't use to (used not to) 4. used to 5. used to/ would 6. sometimes used to/ would sometimes 7. used to 8. Did he use to (Used he to) 9. often used to/ would often 10. didn't use to (used not to) 11. used to

***4/*** 1. My husband would sometimes buy me flowers. 2. Many animals won't usually come out until after dark. 3. We would occasionally go out for lunch. 4. I won't ever drink if I'm driving. 5. When I was a little boy I would always walk to school. 6. Cats won't generally play with dogs. 7. He wouldn't usually speak unless he was spoken to. 8. A rhinoceros will normally run faster than a horse.

***5/*** 1. … 'I'd rather stay … 2. They'd rather die … 3. Would you rather play … 4. I hear you'd rather not discuss … 5. … 'I'd rather not.' 6. We'd rather you left us alone. 7. I'd rather the government spent … 8. We'd rather they didn't make … 9. Her parents would rather she studied harder. 10. … 'We'd rather you didn't.'

## 14 L'infinitif

***1/*** 1. …what to do. 3. … wish to make … 5. … late to start … 6. … not to ask … 9. … want to come …; … prefer to walk … 12. … trying to do … 13. … not to see … 15. … enough to do … 16. … beginning to understand … 19. … like to invite …

***2/*** 1. to be smoking 2. to be repainted 3. to have left 4. to be visiting 5. not to be opened 6. not to have passed 7. to be living 8. have taken 9. not be drunk

***3/***

**A** 1. … the shop to buy … 2. … bathroom to wash … 3. … the optician to get … 4. … phone my husband to tell …

**B** 5. … to them in order to/ so as to invite … 6. … the truth in order not to/ so as not to worry … 7. … now in order not to/ so as not to waste … 8. … evening class in order to/ so as to learn … 9. … very quietly in order not to/ so as not to let me … 10. … very carefully in order not to/ so as not to make … 11. … very early in order to/ so as to miss … 12. … moustache in order not to / so as not to be recognised.

***4/***

**A** 1. We'd like them to meet John. 2. He didn't want her to hear about it. 3. Would you prefer them to speak French? 4. I want everyone to know I love you! 5. They don't like us to use the phone. 6. She would prefer me not to come back. 7. He hates the children to be impolite. 8. We need them to pay us the money. 9. Order him to get the car!

**B** 10. It's essential for him to try to relax. 11. It still isn't clear enough for us to see anything. 12. Wait for the bus to stop. 13. We arranged for her to come on Monday. 14. I can't find anything for them to wear. 15. The piano is for Tom to practise on.

***5/*** 1. hope to 2. refused to 3. 'd love to 4. forgot to 5. like

***6/*** 1. … know how to open it. 2. Could you help us, please? 3. … to have arrived … 4. … to post … 5. We want her to have a good education. 6. I prefer to spend … 7. You'd better hurry up. 8. He promised never to tell anybody. 9. Why not join us? 10. I'll wait for him to call us … 11. Do what you like. I don't care. 12. It's impossible to forget … 13. … made me do! 14. It's too complicated for us to understand. 15. … anything but relax. 16. … in order not to / so as not to dirty … 17. … anything for them to play with?

## 15 *-ed* et *-ing*

***1 /*** 1. fascinating / exciting / interesting 2. excited / annoyed 3. translating 4. annoying 5. shocked 6. bored 7. interested 8. frightening / shocking 9. destroyed 10. interesting / exciting

***2 /*** 1. The match is finished. 2. The car had been stolen. 3. I was lying on my bed. 4. Why are you sitting like that? 5. My mother has already arrived. 6. 'Where's Christine?' 'She's *(= has)* gone/left.' 7. 'When did you leave?' 'On Monday.' 8. 'Have you ever been out / gone out with him?' 'No.' 9. He's *(= has)* stayed in bed all day.

***3 /*** 1. skiing 2. Travelling 3. saying 4. spending 5. cleaning 6. surfing 7. buying 8. interrupting 9. shouting 10. repairing 11. laughing 12. telling

***4 /*** *(Exemples)* 1. I'm looking forward *to* visiting Japan next summer. 2. I sometimes walk to work *instead of* driving. 3. I'm used *to* getting up early. 4. I often talk *about* eating less. 5. I object *to* having to pay for the royal family. 6. I'm fed up *with* trying to look younger than I am. 7. I prefer spending money *to* keeping it in the bank. 8. I always listen to the radio *before* going to sleep. 9. I'm not looking forward *to* being forty. 10. I often feel really happy *without* knowing why. 11. I'll never get used *to* not eating meat. 12. I always feel a little sad *after* finishing a good book.

***5 /*** 1. After finishing the housework, ... 2. ... before seeing it. 3. ... without asking my permission. 4. ... after seeing the film. 5. Before seeing these examples ... 6. ... after knowing each other ... 7. ... before having his coffee. 8. ... without moving your lips!

***6 /*** 1. The man walking towards us ... 2. Did you hear the baby crying? 3. ... caught her driving too fast ... 4. ... road going down to the river. 5. Can you smell something burning? 6. I love to hear birds singing. 7. ... full of happily smiling children / children smiling happily.

***7 /*** 1. I'm not interested ... 2. Skiing is not ... 4. ... worth considering? 5. ... no use pretending ... 7. ... used to speaking ... 8. ... before talking ... 9. ... sound of breaking glass. *(Les phrases 3 et 6 sont correctes.)*

## 16 Infinitif ou *-ing*

***1 /*** 1. would you like to drink 2. I'd like 3. Do you like / Would you like 4. Would you like to have 5. I don't like sitting / to sit 6. Don't you like getting / to get 7. I like staying / to stay 8. doesn't like

***2 /*** 1. looking 2. to work / working 3. discussing 4. to talk 5. watching 6. forgetting 7. to leave / leaving 8. wasting 9. to visit 10. to dance / dancing 11. trying 12. to finish / finishing 13. thinking 14. to work 15. missing 16. to meet

***3 /*** 1. of forgetting 2. to read / of reading 3. to pay 4. asking 5. meeting 6. to go 7. playing 8. talking 9. give 10. put / (putting) 11. to get 12. eating 13. (from) laughing 14. to find 15. calling

***4 /*** 1. drawing, painting 2. to tell 3. keeping 4. to send 5. regaining 6. calling 7. to miss 8. working 9. to turn 10. travelling *(AZ 275)* 11. for being 12. waiting 13. to come 14. hearing 15. raining 16. turning 17. to speak 18. happening 19. living

## 17 Les temps des verbes : présent

***1/*** 1. He plays … 2. You don't worry … 3. She usually tries hard … 4. Why do they hope …? 5. He doesn't brush his teeth … 6. I go … 7. When does the train leave? 8. We don't miss … 9. Does he go …? 10. They don't study …

***2/*** 1. is opening 2. is climbing 3. is moving 4. are you feeling 5. 'm feeling 6. 'm examining 7. 'm walking 8. Are your instruments functioning *(Voir AZ 275.)* 9. 're not getting / aren't getting 10. 'm looking at
11. 'm going back
12. are becoming
13. are going up
14. isn't functioning
15. is approaching 16. 's holding
17. 's happening

***3/*** 1. are things going 2. work / 'm working 3. 's playing 4. Does he practise 5. gives 6. do you like 7. snows 8. miss 9. Do you ski 10. ski 11. enjoy 12. are you working 13. 'm writing 14. do you speak 15. speak 16. travel 17. need 18. do you remember

***4/*** *(Phrases possibles)* 1. I have a shower every morning. 2. I'm meeting my boyfriend tomorrow evening. 3. I often cook spaghetti. 4. I'm doing this exercise at the moment. 5. I go swimming when I have time. 6. I'm going on holiday on Saturday.

***5/*** 3. Right now he doubts everything you tell him. 7. I don't see why we have to do it. 9. Who do you think you are?

***6/*** *(Exemples)* I'm always breaking things. My sister is always causing trouble. My dad is always using bad language. Peter is always talking about himself. My manager is always making cruel remarks.

## 18 Les temps des verbes : passé

***1/*** built, built ; chose, chosen ; came, come ; fell, fallen ; felt, felt ; went, gone / been *(AZ 160)* ; hid, hidden ; left, left ; made, made ; paid, paid ; ran, run ; sold, sold ; sent, sent ; showed, shown ; stole, stolen ; taught, taught ; thought, thought ; threw, thrown ; woke, woken ; wrote, written

***2/*** 1. was taking 2. saw 3. was wearing 4. was carrying 5. was getting 6. ran 7. shouted 8. was ringing 9. was looking 10. was happening 11. went 12. was crying 13. arrived

***3/*** 1. He left the company last May. 2. We've already visited Ireland. 3. I'm very sorry to tell you (that) your father has died. 4. War broke out in 1939. 5. My parents haven't moved to London yet. 6. I've never seen him at the golf club. 7. Have they finished their homework yet? 8. When did his sister work in Germany? 9. We didn't meet her husband at Sarah's dinner party. 10. I can't open the door because I've lost my key. 11. He had a lot of girlfriends when he was at university.

***4/*** 1. They've worked for this company since 1989. 2. You haven't talked to her for two days. 3. She visited her mother three weeks ago. 4. He hasn't written to me since April. 5. I've known him for twenty years. 6. We haven't had a world war since 1945. 7. You cooked dinner five days ago. 8. We haven't been to the cinema for six months.

***5/*** 1. It's been snowing for two hours. 2. She's been playing tennis. 3. The baby has been crying since three o'clock this morning. 4. I've been learning Spanish for a month. 5. Bob has been doing the washing-up. 6. Sarah has been living in Marseilles since March. 7. My father has been reading the newspaper.

***6/*** 1. 've been looking 2. hasn't been feeling 3. Have ... been working 4. I've been trying 5. have ... been working 6. 've been 7. Have ... been playing 8. has known

***7/*** 1. She had just finished her breakfast. 2. She had been reading the newspapers since 9.00 am. 3. She hadn't started to make her phonecalls yet. 4. She had just begun to write her letters. 5. She had been having lunch since 1.00 pm. 6. She had been in town for two hours. 7. She had just got dressed. 8. She had been eating since 9.00 pm. 9. She had been asleep for four hours.

***8/*** 1. Have you been waiting; 've been standing; agreed/ had agreed; said; weren't listening; did; 've had
2. was the man wearing; was raining; couldn't; was he doing; saw; was trying; was using; were you standing; was putting; Did you hear; was listening
3. has she been; joined; has worked/ has been working; came; had she done; hadn't enjoyed/ didn't enjoy; Has she had; arrived; 's been working/ 's worked

## 19 Les temps des verbes : futur

***1/*** 1. will 2. wouldn't 3. 'll (will) 4. would 5. 'll (will) 6. won't 7. 'd (would) 8. won't

***2/*** 1. I think it's going to rain this afternoon. 2. I'm going to pass my driving test before my next birthday. 3. I'm going to stop smoking before the end of this year. 4. I'm going to get a better job one of these days. 5. I'm not going to get married again. 6. I'm never going to be rich. 7. I hope the government is not going to put up taxes. 8. I hope there isn't going to be a nuclear disaster before the year 2000.

***3/*** 1. 'm playing 2. arrives 3. 're leaving 4. Are ... coming 5. have 6. 's phoning 7. are ... going 8. does ... take off 9. is ... meeting

***4/*** 1. they'll call 2. I'll tell 4. we'll go 5. Will you make 6. I'll get 7. will help 8. Shall we take 10. I'll give

***5/*** 1. Would/ Will 2. will 3. would/ will 4. would/ will 5. will/ would 6. wouldn't 7. won't 8. would/ will

***6/*** 1. After three months' they will have seen four countries.
2. By the beginning of May they will have been to the pyramids. *(Pour* been*, voir AZ 160.)*
3. By the end of July they will have been travelling for seven months.
4. In eight months' time they will have visited eleven countries.
5. By the middle of September they will have returned home to Ireland.

***7/*** 1. She'll be seeing Joe Richards. 2. She'll be interviewing her new secretary. 3. She'll be discussing the new brochure with Peter. 4. She'll be phoning John Brown. 5. She'll be reading some business reports. 6. She'll be having lunch with Sarah Johnson.

***8/*** 1. is to 2. was to 3. was to 4. were to 5. are to 6. is to 7. are to 8. are not to

***9/*** 1. 'She's just about to leave now.' 2. 'I was just about to open it.' 3. 'They're just about to go to bed now.' 4. 'Sorry, he was just about to have his dinner.' 5. 'I'm just about to write to her now.' 6. 'We were just about to go home.' 7. 'He's just about to phone him now.'

***10/*** 1. ... they would win their match. 2. ... he was going to give up smoking. 3. ... the plane didn't take off until 12.30. 4. ... she was doing an exam in the morning. 5. ... we were to stay here? 6. ... they were going to move to Australia. 7. ... my music lesson finished at 6.15. 8. … the Prime Minister was to visit Liverpool in April. 9. … he'd be all right. 10. … they were coming on Saturday?

***11 /*** 1. 's going to snow; 'll get; Shall I get; 're going to need/ 'll need
2. starts; 'm meeting; 'll ring; 'll organise; shall I phone; 'll be; 'll talk; is coming
3. 'll never speak; will; 'm not going to tell/ won't tell; will you help; won't
4. shall we do; Shall we take; won't start; 'll call; Shall I ask; Will/ Would you tell; 'll phone
5. does the bus go; 'm going to have/ 'll have; Will you get; Shall I buy; I won't be

***12 /*** 1. will have finished 2. Will you be needing 3. are to 4. 'll be flying 5. was (just) about to 6. wasn't going 7. is to 8. wouldn't forget 9. will have used 10. are about to 11. were going 12. Will you have decided

## 20 Le passif

***1 /*** 1. to be used 2. I am being taught 3. you are chosen 4. he was killed 5. she was being called 6. we have been taken 7. they had been eaten 8. I will be met 9. it would be broken 10. you will have been brought 11. she would have been forgotten 12. being heard

***2 /*** 1. Radioactivity was discovered by Marie and Pierre Curie at the end of the $19^{th}$ century. 2. Is Spanish spoken in Brazil? 3. The money has already been spent. 4. Workers will soon be replaced by robots. 5. How many people are killed on the roads every year? 6. When are you being interviewed/ are you going to be interviewed/ will you be interviewed tomorrow? 7. The Eiffel Tower was built in 1889 by Gustave Eiffel. 8. Cheese is made from milk. 9. He has not been seen since 1985. 10. Your car is being repaired at the moment.

***3 /*** 1. My dinner got eaten by the cat. 2. It'll get stolen if you are not careful! 3. We always get asked to the Christmas party. 4. Have you ever got arrested? 5. All the windows had got broken.

***4 /*** 1. I was given a wonderful prize. 2. You'll be lent £1,000. 3. Nicole has been bought a new car 4. They had been promised promotion. 5. We are taught German on Tuesday evenings. 6. You've been forbidden to leave. 7. I'm very often asked to read my poems. 8. John had been told to stay at home. 9. You'll be asked to play the guitar. 10. They were made to come very early.

***5 /*** 1. was asked; weren't allowed; Were you made; was invited; did you get asked; was shown; was expected; was recorded; will the results be announced; 've been announced
2. 've been sent; 'll get picked up; 'll be driven; 'll get met; 'll be served; 'll get taken; 'll be invited; will we be expected/ (are we expected)
3. got burgled; had been broken; had been disconnected; was stolen; got taken; were damaged; has been burgled; Has anyone been caught; haven't been told

## 21 La phrase : structures de base

***1 /*** 1. When did you get here? 2. How did you travel? 3. Have you been to Paris before? 4. Do you speak French? 5. Where are you staying? 6. Where do they live? 7. Have you been up the Eiffel Tower? 8. Do you like French food? 9. What are you going to do next? 10. How long are you / will you be staying in Paris? 11. What do you do? 12. Would you like to have coffee with me?

**2 /** 1. didn't 2. Haven't 3. doesn't 4. Aren't 5. Didn't 6. Isn't 7. didn't 8. Don't 9. Hasn't

**3 /** 1. How long are you staying here? 2. How high is Mont Blanc? 3. How long had he been ill? 4. How long is the Great Wall of China? 5. How long have they been playing computer games? 6. How wide is the Suez Canal? 7. How often do you see each other? 8. How far is the Sun from the Earth? 9. How many times have you been skiing? 10. How far is the nearest garage? 11. How tall is she? 12. How cold is it?

**4 /** 1. She doesn't eat chocolate. *(AZ 307)* 2. I don't like her. *(AZ 307)* 3. He's never at home. 4. I never go to the seaside during the winter. 5. We don't see Tom at weekends. 6. They don't know everything/anything. 7. He doesn't say hello to everybody/anybody. 8. We drink neither tea nor coffee. 9. She can hardly stand up. 10. You hardly ever visit your mother. 11. I hardly spend any time with him. 12. They finished the exercises without any difficulty.

**5 /** 1. Stop / Don't start 2. Eat 3. Never drink 4. Always brush 5. Don't forget / Remember 6. Remember / Don't forget 7. Always get 8. Don't eat 9. Never go out 10. Stay; live

**6 /** 1. Let's have a drink. 2. Let's try somewhere else. 3. Let's not catch a bus. Let's take a taxi. 4. Let's go home. 5. Let's not go home yet. Let's have some fun.

**7 /** 1. What beautiful eyes! 2. How awful! 3. What a sad life! 4. What terrible luck! 5. What a nice sister you have! 6. How annoying this is! 7. She didn't realise what a kind man he was. 8. Have you noticed how quiet it is?

**8 /** 1. Isn't that a fantastic car! 2. Hasn't she got beautiful hair! 3. Don't those cakes look delicious! 4. Haven't you been wonderful! 5. Wasn't he charming! 6. Won't it be exciting! 7. Hasn't this town changed! 8. Aren't you proud of your children! 9. Didn't they show great courage! 10. Doesn't she sing well!

**9 /** 1. How difficult is this? 2. How hard they are working! 3. How lucky have you been? 4. How interesting it was! 5. How easy is it going to be? 6. How well they played! 7. How quickly do you do it? 8. How busy she is! 9. How beautiful will it look? 10. How nice the weather has been!

**10 /** 1. There is; there are 2. there's going to be / there will be 3. There used to be 4. There was; there were / there have been 5. there will be / there's going to be; there might be 6. There has been; there have been 7. There must be 8. there would be

**11 /** 1. There weren't a lot of/ many people. 2. Might there be a problem with this? 3. There won't be snow in the mountains. 4. Has there been a revolution in Pakistan? 5. There shouldn't be more help for the poor. 6. Would there be an ecological disaster if this nuclear power station exploded? 7. There didn't use to be/ used not to be a cinema in this town. 8. Are there going to be too many people at the party? 9. There aren't a lot of/ many cars on the island. 10. Was there a good film on TV last night? 11. There haven't been many complaints against the hospital.

## 22 Tags : question tags, reprises interrogatives, réponses courtes

**1 /** 1. You're 31 years old, aren't you? 2. You don't come from London, do you? 3. You aren't married, are you? 4. You've been living with your girlfriend since January, haven't you?

5. She's been away for the last few weeks, hasn't she? 6. You haven't got a job at the moment, have you? / You don't have ..., do you?
7. You were in the army five years ago, weren't you? 8. You can use a gun, can't you? 9. You've never been in prison, have you?
10. You were in The Red Lion pub last night, weren't you? 11. It was after 10.30, wasn't it? 12. Tony Smith was with you, wasn't he?
13. He didn't give you anything, did he? 14. You're going to stay / You're staying in town for the next few weeks, aren't you?

***2/*** 1. will you? 2. shall we?
3. don't you? 4. didn't you?
5. didn't he? 6. didn't it? 7. didn't you? 8. didn't he? *(AZ 170)*
9. didn't he? 10. don't you?
11. aren't I? 12. will you?

***3/*** 2. e 3. f 4. a 5. h 6. i
7. b 8. d 9. g

***4/***
**A** 1. e 2. a 3. d 4. c 5. b
**B** 1. d 2. a 3. f 4. g
5. a/c 6. e 7. b

***5/*** 1. 'Nor me.'/ 'I can't either.'/ 'Neither/Nor can I.' 2. 'Me too.'/ 'I am too.'/ 'So am I.' 3. 'Me too.'/ 'I do too.'/ 'So do I.' 4. 'Nor me.'/ 'I haven't either.'/ 'Neither/ Nor have I.' 5. 'Nor me.'/ 'I'm not either.'/ 'Neither/ Nor am I.'
6. 'Nor me.'/ 'I wouldn't either.'/ 'Neither/ Nor would I.' 7. 'Me too./ 'I will too.'/ 'So will I.' 8. 'Me too.'/ ' I am too.'/ 'So am I.' 9. 'Me too'/ 'I have too.'/ 'So have I.' 10. 'Nor me.'/ 'I won't either.'/ 'Neither/ Nor will I.' 11. 'Me too.'/ 'I do too.'/ 'So do I.'

## 23 Discours indirect

***1/*** 1. She told us she had dreamed about becoming President for a long time. 2. Every new President says it's the start of a new age. 3. She promised that there would be great changes.
4. She doesn't think they will need to increase taxes. 5. All politicians say they're going to conquer inflation. 6. She said they were going to bring down unemployment. 7. She told us she had always been against nuclear weapons. 8. She said she wanted to bring peace to the world.
9. She promised that she would do her best for the country.
10. She asked us to work with her for a better future! 11. She told us never to lose hope.

***2/*** 1. 'We/ You must all work together.' 2. 'It may/ might be difficult at times.' 3. 'We/ You should be strong.' 4. 'We/ You shouldn't give up hope.' 5. 'You ought to give me your support.'
6. 'You can count on me.'

***3/*** 1. I asked her if/ whether it was really the happiest day of her life. 2. I asked her what sort of changes she was planning.
3. I asked her if/ whether she would reduce taxation. 4. I asked her if/ whether she could really conquer inflation. 5. I asked her what she was going to do about unemployment. 6. I asked her how long she had been against nuclear weapons. 7. I asked her if/ whether she would really bring peace to the world. 8. I asked her how the future would be better.
9. I asked her if/ whether she saw difficult times in the years to come.
10. I asked her how hopeful she was.

***4/*** 1. I told Tom (that) he was an idiot. 2. He asked me if I wanted the books. 3. We asked them what they were doing the next day.
4. His wife told me (that) he hadn't been at work the week before.
5. She asked them if he still lived there. 6. I asked her where she had been the day before. 7. They told him (that) they had phoned him two days before. 8. They asked her if he was going to Paris the following week.

***5/*** 1. They said nothing to me.

2. They told him to leave them alone. 4. What did they tell you? 7. Tell him before he goes. 8. They said (to us) (that) there was a problem. *(Say et tell ne peuvent pas être inversés dans les autres phrases.)*

***6 /*** 1. She told him / said (that) she couldn't come to the concert on Tuesday. 2. He asked her why she hadn't told him before. 3. She told him / said (that) she had been very busy. 4. He said / told her (that) he had bought the tickets two weeks before. 5. She told him / said (that) Tony might like to go. 6. He said / told her (that) he'd prefer to go with her. 7. She said / told him (that) she had to travel to Paris on business. *(Pour* had to, *voir AZ 172.)* 8. He asked her when she was leaving. 9. She said / told him (that) she was flying on Tuesday morning. 10. He asked her if she was staying for long. 11. She said / told him (that) she should be back the following week. 12. He asked her if she would send him a postcard. 13. She asked him if he would phone her in Paris. 14. He asked/told her to bring him back a bottle of cognac.

## 24 *If, unless* et *whether*

***1 /*** *(Combinaisons possibles)*

1. i / l
2. c / f
3. a / b / e / g / h
4. k
5. c / i / j / l
6. b / g / h
7. c / d / l
8. l
9. a / e / g
10. a / b / g / h
11. c
12. e / g

***2 /*** *(Phrases possibles)* 1. He would have gone with his girlfriend if they hadn't broken up just before the holiday. 2. He wouldn't have gone with his brother, Paul, if there had been anybody / somebody else free at the time. 3. They would have cycled everywhere if Tom hadn't hurt his leg. 4. They would have camped a lot if the weather hadn't been awful / had been better / OK. 5. They would have visited lots of interesting places if Paul hadn't fallen ill. 6. They would have stayed for two weeks if they hadn't spent all their money after ten days.

***3 /*** 1. If you would inform/tell your wife that we are waiting for her downstairs… 2. I wondered if they'd arrive on time. 3. We don't know if we'll be free tomorrow. 4. Do you want to come with me? If so, hurry up! 5. Have we (got) enough wine? If not, I'll buy another few (a few more) bottles. 6. We'll stay here if necessary. 7. If I were you I wouldn't say a word to them. 8. If you should get lost, don't hesitate to telephone us.

***4 /*** 1. … here unless the weather improves … 2. Unless we hurry, … 3. … in the sun unless I'm wearing … 4. … remember whether you … 5. Unless you make an effort, … 6. … tell whether they're boys or girls! 7. … contacts me unless there's … 8. … by train unless they can … 9. Ask them whether they want …

***5 /*** 1. comes; 'll; if / whether; If not; Unless; whether
2. didn't; 'd; was; would
3. had known; would never have got
4. should; was / were; would
5. If; will

## 25 Autres conjonctions

***1 /*** 1. will; make; will be; move
2. is; comes; will; will
3. get; will; get

***2 /*** 1. gets 2. talks 3. calls 4. want 5. have done 6. have eaten 7. have completed 8. stopped 9. changed 10. had asked 11. had had

12. had finished

***3/*** 1. It's been raining since Thursday. 2. She's lived in Australia since she was a child/ since her childhood. 3. He's not seen her since he started university/ since he's been at university. 4. We haven't played football since we were at school/ since we left school. 5. I hadn't visited my aunt since I was ten.

***4/*** 1. It's five weeks since I had a letter from him. 2. It's a long time since you looked so well. 3. It's more than a month since they last talked to each other. 4. It was over fifteen years since I had worked with him. 5. It was days since the children had had a proper meal.

***5/*** 1. so that 2. while 3. until 4. in case 5. even though 6. as 7. whereas/while 8. as if 9. provided that 10. as long as

***6/*** 1. until; is 2. Although/ While 3. as long as; can 4. since 5. Although/ Though 6. in order that; shouldn't/ wouldn't get 7. as long as/ so long as; don't make 8. as though 9. in case; feels/ should feel 10. though 11. in spite of

## 26 L'ordre des mots

***1/*** 1. We usually spend ... 2. He is probably talking ... 3. We were also very pleased. 4. I have just heard ... 5. You rarely visit ... 6. Never take drugs. 7. They are both doctors. 8. She hardly ever rang me. 9. We are certainly going to complain. 10. They have nearly finished ... 11. It was mainly a financial question. 12. ... he would still have been unhappy.

***2/*** 1. When did you last see them? 2. I certainly don't know him. 3. Do you always wear that hat? 4. She didn't even say hello. 5. Has he really lost it? 6. They probably aren't coming. 7. Can she only speak English? 8. Are you still going to live in London?

***3/*** 1. We don't swim very much in the winter. 2. I don't eat meat at all. 3. Perhaps we were talking too much. 4. He always used to play tennis very well. 5. They travel to the USA a lot. 6. Maybe she couldn't get a babysitter. 7. I very much prefer eating at home to going out to eat. 8. He was at a meeting in Bordeaux yesterday. 9. I'll ring you at home later. 10. Did you sleep well last night? 11. We worked together very successfully at the Oxford branch in 1987. 12. They fell very much in love in Greece last summer.

***4/*** 1. ... enough wine ... 2. ... half a bottle ... 3. ... quite a good teacher. 4. I rather like walking ... 5. ... rather a difficult decision. 6. ... such a good time.

***5/*** 1. Try not to wake the dog up! 4. We looked up the words in the dictionary. 5. Could you turn the TV down a bit, please? 7. She wrote down her address and gave it to him.

***6/*** 1. She's been teaching my children German for over a year. 2. Please, would you tell a story to Sarah? 4. She offered my father a job. 6. They showed their house to us. 7. Did you give them the keys? 9. I'll send the details to you tomorrow.

***7/*** 1. Should anything go wrong, please ... 2. No sooner had I got into the bath than the phone ... 3. Only then did he realise he had left ... 4. At no time (in my life) have I ever regretted ... 5. Were I in his position, I would not stay ... 6. Not only did they arrive late, but they did not even ... 7. Only after her mother's death did she find out ... 8. Hardly had we left the house when it ... 9. Had they told me there was a problem, I would certainly have helped them.

***8 /*** 1. Those are the chocolates that my mother loves. 2. Do you know what your father wants? 3. You made my sister cry. 4. Did you ask what time the match starts? 5. I don't understand the decisions that the government makes. 6. Can you tell me where the Smith family lives? 7. We saw two men and a woman with a baby get into the car. 8. I didn't hear the car drive away. 9. That's the office where my father works. 10. Don't let the rain get in! 11. Perhaps it is not too late.

***9 /*** 1. What did your friend die of last year? 2. Here's the photo you were looking for. 3. It's not a very interesting town to live in. 4. No one likes being laughed at. 5. That's the illness my mum suffered from all her life. 6. Who have they been waiting for all this time? 7. There's nothing to worry about. 8. This problem has already been taken care of.

***10 /*** 1. We seldom go to the cinema. 2. He is hardly twelve years old. 3. You have all had your difficulties. 4. They did not even phone us! 5. You certainly don't do it that way. 6. Perhaps she's not very interested in rugby. 7. I don't speak French very well. 8. We used to enjoy dancing a lot. 9. You spoke very passionately at the meeting yesterday. 10. She's not strong enough to carry it. 11. Have we got enough ice cream? 12. Half my books were stolen. 13. See you in half an hour! 14. That's quite an interesting opinion. 15. We rather like jazz. 16. It's such a wonderful restaurant. 17. You're such a nice girl! 18. Take them off immediately! 19. Explain the rules to me, will you? 20. Not only had I forgotten their address, but … 21. Ask her what she wants. 22. This is the poem that Tom wrote. 23. Did you hear someone speak? 24. Where did your father come from?

## 27 Les prépositions

***1 /*** 1. to 2. for 3. from 4. in 5. Ø 6. by 7. for 8. with 9. for 10. about 11. into 12. Ø; Ø 13. about 14. of 15. from 16. Ø 17. on/off 18. Ø 19. of 20. at

***2 /*** 1. In; on 2. on; on 3. on; on 4. In; by 5. on; in 6. at; in

***3 /*** 1. at; in; to; Ø 2. in; in; in; into 3. at; on 4. in; in; to; in 5. to; at; Ø 6. in; On 7. to 8. to 9. at 10. Ø; to 11. into; on 12. onto

***4 /*** 1. about 2. after that / then 3. about ten days 4. first 5. about 6. by the end of the week 7. about 8. By the time she rings me 9. What about going 10. afterwards / after that

***5 /*** 1. According to his / her doctor 2. up to 80 hours a week 3. opposite you 4. from 9 o'clock to 11 o'clock 5. In my opinion / I think 6. with his parents 7. in front of the house 8. From tomorrow onwards 9. to the edge of the universe 10. She's gone home. 11. down to the end of the first paragraph 12. from an old lady 13. in Racine 14. up to the age of 70

***6 /*** 1. across 2. in front of 3. while 4. through 5. for 6. before 7. to

## 28 Les mots de liaison

***1 /*** *au contraire* – on the contrary
*au fait* – by the way
*au moins* – at least
*autrement dit* – in other words
*bref* – in a word
*d'ailleurs* – besides
*d'après moi* – in my opinion / I think
*d'après Paul* – according to Paul
*d'un autre côté* – on the other hand
*d'un côté* – in a way
*dans l'ensemble* – on the whole
*en fait* – actually
*en tout cas* – anyway
*pour moi* – I think / in my opinion
*pourtant* – yet

*quant à Paul* – as for Paul
*remarque* – mind you
*sinon* – otherwise
*tout de même* – all the same

***2 /*** 1. as 2. Either 3. so 4. neither 5. As 6. both 7. either 8. as 9. both 10. like 11. Neither 12. also

***3 /*** 1. whatever 2. Whenever 3. Whichever 4. However 5. whoever 6. wherever 7. however 8. Whatever 9. wherever 10. Whoever 11. whenever 12. Whichever

## 29 Comment traduire ...?

***1 /*** 1. I must write to my mother this evening. 2. We'll need six more chairs. 3. You must come on time! 4. It took ten years to build it. 5. It'll take two days to finish this work. 6. This book isn't interesting enough. 7. They lack the necessary money. 8. I missed my parents a lot. 9. Hurry up! You're going to miss the bus! 10. You'll like this hotel, I think. 11. Did they like us? 12. I didn't enjoy/like the concert at all.

***2 /*** 1. There are two solutions to this problem. 2. They got married ten years ago. 3. She hasn't written to me for six weeks.
4. I stopped smoking a long time ago. 5. She's lived/ been living in Paris for a long time. 6. Your father is looking for you. 7. A man was looking at me. 8. Someone has forgotten a shoe/ one of their shoes. 9. Some schoolchildren are very difficult. 10. A lot of people are killed on the roads each year.

***3 /*** 1. My husband makes me drive very slowly. 2. Make them wash their hands. 3. Don't make her cry. 4. They have/ get the carpets cleaned every year.
5. You must have/ get the tyre replaced. 6. She's had her hair cut. 7. We're going to have/ get central heating installed. 8. I make my children do the washing up.
9. Our parents used to make us get up very early. 10. I'm having/ getting a small house built in the country.

***4 /*** 1. 'I'm going to kill them,' said Sophie, picking up a big knife.
2. While waiting at the bus stop Pierre witnessed a car accident.
3. When she opened the door she recognised the man immediately.
4. While he was cooking he burned his finger. 5. 'How can I persuade her to stay?' 'By asking her to forgive you.' 6. He ran upstairs. 7. 'Don't leave me,' she said, crying. 8. As I was introducing him I forgot his name!
9. If you work hard, you'll pass your exams. 10. On her way to the office my mother dropped her umbrella.

## 30 La grammaire des mots

***1 /*** 1. He wishes he had a car.
2. I wish I didn't have to go to work every day. 3. We/ I wish we hadn't got married when we were teenagers. 4. She wishes she hadn't spent all her money on new clothes. 5. I wish you would hurry up. 6. I wish you would write to me more often. 7. We/ I hope you'll visit us again next year.
8. I hope I'll have some time tomorrow. 9. They wish they didn't live in the city. 10. I wish I had gone to university. 11. I wish you would stop criticising my work.
12. I hope he'll telephone me at the weekend.

***2 /*** 1. Let's get another bottle of wine!
2. Get up! You're going to be/ You'll be late!
3. I was getting tired and I was getting hungry
4. They got lost in the snow.
5. When did you get divorced?
6. Fortunately, nobody got killed.
7. He tried to get them to hurry.
8. I can't get my husband to understand this.

9. She couldn't get the car to start.

***3 /*** 1. We didn't agree with their decision. 2. He asked me my nationality. 3. Ask Paul for the key, and ask him the way to the house. 4. Have you explained the situation to the children? 5. I'll explain to you what you must do. 6. He suggested another date to us. 7. Can you suggest to Ann that she comes on Tuesday evening? 8. I suggested (that) they (should) take the exam next year. 9. We suggest going by bus. 10. I often think of/about my holidays. 11. What do you think of this music? 12. I thought (that) I'd find her in the office, but she had already left. 13. They don't think (that) they'll have enough time to do it. 14. I'm thinking of inviting Richard to dinner this weekend. 15. Why do you want to learn English? 17. His parents want him to become a doctor, but he doesn't want to. 18. She would like to find/get a job, but her husband doesn't want her to. He wants her to stay at home with the children. 19. 'Can I leave the documents here?' 'As you like.'

## 31 Mots à ne pas confondre

1. listen to *(AZ 173)*
2. still *(AZ 387)*
3. as; than *(AZ 381)*
4. used to; 'm used to *(AZ 393, 395)*
5. 's dead; died *(AZ 98)*
6. dead man *(AZ 98)*
7. died *(AZ 98)*
8. How; what; what *(AZ 180)*
9. here *(AZ 175)*
10. remind *(AZ 345)*
11. journey *(AZ 389)*
12. trip *(AZ 389)*
13. feel; fell *(AZ 241)*
14. leave; live *(AZ 241)*
15. quiet; quite *(AZ 241)*
16. economic *(AZ 241)*
17. expect *(AZ 410)*
18. take *(AZ 68)*

Maquette intérieure : **G. Brevière**
Mise en pages : **N. Grimaud**

*Imprimé en France* par l'Imprimerie Hérissey - 27000 Évreux (Eure)
Dépôt légal : 37817 - septembre 2003 - N° d'impression : 95565